T5-BAO-776

African-American Young Men Transitions towards Independent Living

African-American Young Men Transitions towards Independent Living

A Case Study

Odeather Allen Hill, Ph.D., ACSW, CSW

VANTAGE PRESS
New York

FIRST EDITION

All rights reserved, including the right of
reproduction in whole or in part in any form.

Copyright © 1998 by Odeather Allen Hill, Ph.D., ACSW, CSW

Published by Vantage Press, Inc.
516 West 34th Street, New York, New York 10001

Manufactured in the United States of America
ISBN: 0-533-12291-0

Library of Congress Catalog Card No.: 97-90111

0 9 8 7 6 5 4 3 2 1

Thank you is extended to my mother, Willie Lee Allen, and my father, James Allen, for giving me to this world. Thank you, Grandmama Martha Alexander, who raised me since I was five years old. Grandmama, I have always remembered you telling me to go as far in the educational arena as possible. Although neither of you is alive to help the obtainer of the degree, Doctor of Philosophy, I know that you are with me in spirit.

Thank you to my dearest friend, Edgar Jerome Dew, Esq., who would often ask me the question, "Odeather, when are you going to get a Ph.D.?" Well, Mr. Dew, I have finally arrived. Thanks for your encouragement.

To my darling children and grandchildren, who have spoken so proudly to their friends, thank you, Undra, Angula, Zetrick, Elaine, and grandchildren Andrew, Nikki, Denise, Aireal, Darian, Aaron, and Autumn.

Nothing is more rewarding than a man who believes that he is independent, has a sense of self-empowerment, demonstrates self-reliance, demands respect from others and gives respect to others.
—Odeather Allen Hill, Ph.D., ACSW, CSW

Contents

Foreword

Many young African-American men making a transition toward adulthood have had experiences grounded and shaped by adverse environmental barriers, circumstances, and realities as seen by them within today's society. Barriers such as inadequate economic resources, discrimination, social and judicial injustices and intimidation, help to shape the psychological adjustment and behavioral attitudes of many young African-American men. When these men are faced with such barriers, their efforts to achieve transition to independent status are fragmented and oftentimes interrupted and delayed. In these instances, a disproportionate number of young African-American men are forced to seek illegal means of securing economic security and a sense of self-empowerment.

To that end, many of these young men are at risk of imprisonment or even death. They become subjects of a society that victimizes them by creating barriers that block their progress. These adverse institutional barriers cause them to experience chronic emotional tension, feelings of mistrust of the larger society, their peers, and their own communities. Similarly, many develop a sense of hopelessness, helplessness, frustration, indifference, and anger. Their feelings are frequently misdirected toward themselves, their peers, and members of their communities. According to A. N. Wilson (1991, pp. 126–127) these young men often behave in an explosive and violent manner against themselves and toward those who are within arm's reach of them, usually those people living in their own environment. Thus, as a result of being faced with adverse institutional barriers as well as self-destructive behavior, these young men are considered to be an endangered species.

I am of the belief that this "diagnosis" of being an endangered species can change with the right strategies and proper support. Strategies important to effect such change include the African-American community collectively and collaboratively, taking a strong stance to protect these young men from adverse oppressive institutional barriers. The African-American community must not only speak about creating an economic base to assist these young men, but they must take necessary action needed to create such economic base, so that these young men can gain and maintain a sense of self-empowerment and financial security. Additionally, the African-American community must provide these men with safe and secure living arrangements and emotional support for the period of time they are practicing independent living. Rather than the African-American community demonstrating fear of these young men, they must act as extended family members. Similarly, they must give individuals a second, third, and fourth chance to overcome the adverse effects experienced as a result of many adverse oppressive institutional barriers.

Based on this belief I developed a program that I chose to call the Supervised Practice Independent Living Skills Training (SPILST) Program. I worked in collaboration with a community agency to increase the chances of four 18-to-20-year-old young African-American men to make the transition from being known to the community as juvenile delinquents, neglected and abused, to that of being known as high school graduates, self-motivated, and productive university students. A case study was conducted to investigate the kinds of adverse institutional barriers these four young men experienced as they made this transition toward independence while participating in transitional living circumstances. The SPILST Program was designed to provide them with opportunities to practice the independent living skills in a small apartment complex while receiving supportive services from a community agency. These young men were responsible for assuming head of household duties while attending school and working. They attended workshops in order to practice daily living activities, such as budgeting, time management, conflict management as well as individual and group counseling on self-esteem and self-advocacy skills.

Each of these young men reported having difficulty in securing employment. They often felt that they were discriminated against and expressed frustration at their sense of power-lessness to address their perceived injustices. Although they expressed disenchantment with school, only one of these young men reported that at an early age he was assigned to special education classes. The "special education" stigma followed him through high school. However, when he received his diploma, he had scored above average on the Scholastic Achievement Test (SAT). One young man experienced violence perpetrated by another African-American youth and one youth experienced police harassment. All of the young men, during the course of the case study, expressed apprehension about their safety in regard to possible Black-on-Black violent acts against them by their peers. Two young men committed acts of aggression and needed the advocacy of the community agency to avoid arrest. When disciplinary problems occurred, rather than the individuals being eliminated from the program, they were given a second and third chance to think about alternative problem-solving strategies. The intervention strategy was not only carefully designed with socialization experiences but also a nurturing and forgiving model. At the conclusion of the program, three of these young men attended college in another geographical area. The fourth young man continued to live in the transitional home after the case study ended.

The findings from this case study were consistent with observations by many social scientists that the transition from adolescence to young adulthood is very difficult for some low-income young men. The void caused by the absence of family and societal support, as well as by advocacy, was filled with the intervention of an independent living training program and support services to enable these young men to develop skills that would enable them to be more self-reliant and independent. One of the most important conclusions drawn from the case study was that despite urban, low-income circumstances and juvenile neglect and abuse experienced by these 18-to-20-year-old African-American men, they could still make the transition toward independent status. Even though these young men were faced with adverse institutional barriers that impeded their efforts to make this transition, they beat the odds. The chances of young

African-American adult males reaching a greater level of independence increased with support from a community agency as well as with provision of safe, supportive, and stable living environment.

The contents of this book are the results of the findings from the case study. This book is crucially important, because it discusses strategies useful to assist young African-American men to make transitions toward independent living. While this book is geared toward young African-American men, it can also be useful for females and males of all races, creeds and national origin. This book provides examples of collaborative efforts between an independent home provider and a community service agency in maximizing resources to help these young people in transition toward independence rather than reinforcing dependency.

Preface

This book evolved out of three years of research and six months of case study, which was conducted as partial fulfillment of a doctoral degree program at the Union Institute in Cincinnati, Ohio. The chapters in this book include the experiences of four young adults who participated in the case study as well as other young adult males as they attempted to achieve independent living. Factors important to helping these young adults reach independent lives will be discussed.

This book is not intended to advocate for reverse racial segregation or discrimination. It is not intended to support non-cooperation among African-Americans and other groups. Nor is it intended to advocate for aggressive behavior of African-Americans against non-African-Americans. It is not intended to condone the negative behavior and attitudes of some young African-American men. Instead this book is intended to advocate for the enhancement of collective economic, psychological, sociopolitical, sociological and community empowerment among African-Americans. It is written to stimulate a different way of thinking regarding these young men. Rather than the African-American community and researchers inadvertently promoting, through their own writings, the thinking that young African-American men are an endangered species, they must promote positive thinking, so that these young adults can have hope for the future. Repeating the words that young African-American men are an endangered species, paints a grim picture for many of them. This sends a psychological message to these young men so that not only do they see themselves in a hopeless and helpless light, but their own communities see them in that dim light as well. The African-American community must realize that the genesis of young African-American men gaining hope that they will live beyond the age of twenty-five, comes from the African-American community. Therefore, the African-American community must speak the words loud and clear for the whole world to hear, that young African-American men are an empowered, productive, and self-reliant species rather than an endangered one. This book is intended to spark a stronger and more consistent interest within the African-American community in building up their own communities; to financially support African-American businesses; to return to the African-American family customs, traditions, values, and cultural orientation. This book advocates for inner-city young African-American men to stop lynching one another through homicidal acts, as well as to stop killing themselves through suicidal acts. Similarly, these young men must stop possessing guns, using drugs, and impregnating young girls.

The purpose of this book is to encourage African-American adults to participate in activities designed to assist young African-American men in making the transition toward independent living. Their communities must continue to advocate against those adverse oppressive institutional factors, such as unemployment, underemployment, adverse educational opportunities, racism, availability of hand guns, and accessibility of illegal drugs. The African-American community must send a message to its young men to lay down their weapons (guns) and pick up the armor of love. They need to make peace with each other, to come together in order to save this and future generations of African-American males. They must know that it is "high time" that they take leadership roles. They must realize that, just as their forefathers created an atmosphere that promoted the belief that their fate was in their own hands, they can, with the support of their communities, guide their own destinies, increase their own economic security, and maintain the well-being of their families. They must learn ways to resist the internalization of negative messages that are designed to oppress, causing them to feel as less than some of the greatest persons in the world. They must not allow adverse oppressive institutional factors to stimulate feelings of disempowerment, anger, and feelings of rage toward themselves and members of their own group. The message in this book is designed to encourage young inner-city African-American men to utilize adverse institutional forces, such as lack of employment and inadequate educational opportunities, as motivators to take positive action toward building a safe, productive, economically empowered, and meaningful community for themselves and future generations.

Acknowledgments

Thanks to my doctoral committee. You have made me reach higher in academic excellence than I ever imagined I could reach. Committee members: Sylvia I. B. Hill, Ph.D., Orian Worden, Ph.D., Melvyn C. Raider, Ph.D., ACSW, Eugene E. Pettis, Ph.D., ACSW, Reginald L. Witherspoon, Ph.D., Marie de Laures Carrena, M.A., and Audrey O. Faulkner, Ph.D., ACSW.

Thanks to the Union Institute for creating such a unique program seemingly designed just for me, flexible, yet structured.

A special thanks to Don Bosco Hall executive staff: Mr. Edward Sutton, Ms. Jo-Anne Woodard, Mr. Lawrence Abner, and other staff members at Don Bosco Hall. To the four participants, thanks a great deal. Also to Andre and Keith for participating in the preliminary interviews.

Without Rheva Gregory and Rhonda Foster, I don't know who would have done the word processing for me, thank you.

Thanks to Aziz Adisa Masai, M.Ed., who took charge of editing, formatting and printing my Program Summary, Transcripts, and Dissertation.

The Honorable Clyde Cleveland, Detroit City Council and Staff. You all have made my internship a meaningful one.

Special thanks to: Dr. Emil A. Birdsong and Dr. Barbara Dorsett and to all of my friends and supporters. Most of all, I thank God for giving me the strength to make it through this long and tiring journey. "Without My God, My Loved Ones and My Friends—I Am Nothing."

Project Demonstrating Excellence Abstract

The purpose of this case study was to investigate the kinds of adverse institutional barriers four African-American adolescents experienced while participating in a transitional living program. The program was designed to provide them with opportunities to practice independent living skills in a small apartment complex while receiving supportive community services from a community agency. Participants were charged with assuming head of household responsibilities while attending school and working. Participants attended workshops in order to practice daily living activities such as budgeting, time management, and conflict management as well as individual and group counseling on self-esteem and self advocacy skills.

Participants in the study were four urban, low-income, African-American adolescents between the ages of 18 and 20 years old. As temporary wards of the State of Michigan because they were in neglectful or abusive family situations, they received monthly stipends. When they were selected to participate in the transitional living program, they were living in a community-based residential facility.

Interviews were conducted with the participants and representatives of the community agency servicing them three times during the six-month duration of the case study. Each of the participants reported having difficulties securing employment. They often felt that they were discriminated against and expressed frustrations at their sense of powerlessness to address their perceived injustices. Although they expressed disenchantment with school, only one participant reported that at an early age he was assigned to special education classes and that the special education stigma followed him during high school.

When he completed high school, however, he scored above average on the Scholastic Achievement Test (SAT). One participant experienced violence perpetrated by another African-American youth and one youth experienced police harassment. All of the youths, during the course of the study, expressed apprehensions about their safety from one or the other potential sources of violence. Two youths committed acts of aggression and needed the advocacy of the community agency to avoid arrest. When disciplinary problems occurred, rather than eliminating the youths from the program, the principal investigator gave them second and third chances to think about alternative problem-solving strategies. The intervention strategy was not only carefully designed with socialization experiences but also a nurturing and forgiving model. At the conclusion of the program, three participants attended college in other geographical areas and one participant continues to live in the transitional home.

The findings of this study were consistent with observations by many social scientists that the transition from adolescence to young adulthood is very difficult for some low-income African-American males. The absence of family and societal support as well as advocacy was made up for by the intervention of an independent living training program and support services to enable participants to develop skills that would enable them to be more self-reliant and live independently. Knowledge acquired from this study, provides examples of youth experiences useful to social workers and human service professionals investigating how institutional factors impede African-American youths as well as providing a model of the role that support services can play as an alternative family support system. This study was also an example of a collaborative effort between an independent home provider and a community-based residential facility to maximize the opportunities for young people to have independent living experiences rather than living experiences that reinforce dependency.

African-American Young Men Transitions towards Independent Living

ONE

Introduction

This qualitative research case study focused on the experiences of four low-income, urban, state juvenile court wards, African-American male adolescents, as they practiced independent living while receiving supportive community program services. For some members of this population, difficulties reaching independent living in urban settings have had historical origins, with highly personal consequences. Institutional factors, such as insufficient financial resources, lack of educational opportunities, and other factors that have impeded their struggle have been documented since the 1800s. Consequently, the nature of the adolescent's struggle to reach independent lifestyles has been an important topic for study in American society and continues to command immediate attention today.

In general, the nature of the struggle of adolescents to reach independence has been a major concern of some human service systems. These systems have influenced society's efforts to set standards for independent living services. One system involved in this effort is the Child Welfare League of America (CWLA), Washington, D.C., which has released the Standards for Independent Living Services. The major goal of the CWLA has been to set standards for practice in all child welfare services. Beginning in 1920 they helped to redefine the responsibility and conditions that encourage individualized growth and development. The CWLA formulated a series of standards based on present knowledge and the developmental needs of children, as well as ways of meeting those specific needs effectively.

The Child Welfare League of America's efforts to redefine the policies and practices that provide the framework of standards for youth work served as an important analytical basis

1

for this researcher's work with youth, particularly with the low-income urban state juvenile court-warded African-American male adolescents. To better serve these adolescents, we cannot overlook the fact that in today's society, social and economic adversities exist within the urban community and institutional systems. The presence of these adversities contributes to the horrendous struggle of low-income urban African-American male adolescents as they attempt to reach independent lifestyles. Those variations of adverse conditions represent the configuration of hardship that these adolescents face. Therefore, to get to the core of the nature of their struggle, the following questions surfaced in the mind of this researcher. These questions were based on the review of past literature and the researcher's past personal and professional experiences.

RESEARCH QUESTIONS

The questions for the study were:

1. How do such adverse institutional factors as unemployment and unequal educational opportunities impede low-income urban state juvenile court-ward African-American male adolescents' efforts to reach independent lifestyles?
2. How do supervised practiced independent living skills training improve the independent living lifestyles of these adolescents?
3. How do public supportive community services assist in the achievement of independent lifestyles for these adolescents?
4. How do advocacy techniques used by the public supportive community agency on the behalf of these adolescents decrease the adverse impact that institutional factors have on their efforts to reach independent living lifestyles?

In an effort to answer these questions, the researcher began to search for current literature that would examine each of the identified institutional factors and to determine their impact.

STATEMENT OF RESEARCH PROBLEM

Research has pointed out that sufficient financial resources, family support, and societal support are important to adolescents assuming young adult roles. Yet, for many urban African-American male adolescents, such resources are often completely absent or limited. These limitations are prevalent when employment opportunities are scarce and when adolescents are poorly educated, poor, and persons of color. Such barriers, according to some researchers, exist too often in the lives of far too many urban African-American male adolescents. However, sufficient research has not been conducted documenting experiences of African-American males as they make transitions to independent young adult roles in society.

NEED FOR RESEARCH STUDY

Donald W. Riegle, Jr., U.S. Senator, State of Michigan, stated in a report, *Plight of African-American Men in Urban America* (1991), that some members of the society had concerns about the adverse conditions faced by many African-American male adolescents. In expressing those concerns in his opening statement on March 19, 1991, at the U.S. Senate Committee on Banking, Housing and Urban Affairs, Washington D.C., Riegle emphasized the importance of examining the magnitude and implications of the barriers that impeded the progress of African-American males in today's society. He indicated that the problems confronting this particular group of urban Americans were profoundly intertwined with an array of problems within American cities, and that this nation is currently in a crisis. Riegle further indicated that these problems included discrimination in educational and employment opportunities. He stated:

> Recent employment statistics for the fourth quarter of 1990 indicated that the U.S. unemployment rate for black males was 19 percent, compared to 7.8 percent for white males. In my home State of Michigan, black male unemployment exceeds 17 percent. In major urban areas, the unemployment figures are even bleaker.

3

Further research uncovered a higher local unemployment rate than that reported nationally. According to D. Gray (1991), in the City of Detroit alone, for 1990, the rate of unemployment for African-American males was 21.3 percent, versus 10.6 percent for their white male counterparts. Supporting Riegle's statement, Gray (1991), indicated that for African-American male adolescents, the unemployment rate was disproportionately higher than for white male adolescents. Gray also observed that unemployment for African-American male adolescents was 48 percent, compared to 25.9 percent for white male adolescents in most urban areas. Such adverse conditions, according to Sum & Fogg (1990), have far-reaching effects. These researchers cited that inadequate educational and economic status decrease African-American males' chances to earn enough money to support their families or make other young adult choices, such as attending college. M. B. Phillips (1991) asserted that such adverse conditions may breed a sense of hopelessness and helplessness.

Similarly, according to A. N. Wilson (1991), far too many African-Americans are kept poor by American institutions. Far too many of these men are neglected by the health care and educational systems. Wilson went on to say that major institutions that are supposedly designed to assist in improving the lives of African-Americans, in too many instances, actually aid and abet the disabling and exploiting of this population. Consistent with Wilson's observation, Gibbs (1988) stated that instead of being supportive, society seemingly has decided to ignore and isolate African-American males in ghettos. Gibbs indicated that the situation appears as if most social scientists and public policy specialists would rather label than analyze and move towards solutions to the underlying causes of many of the apparent self-destructive and dysfunctional behaviors of some African-American male adolescents.

Gibbs also indicated that a great deal of emphasis has been placed on "blaming the victims for their own victimization," blaming them for the consequences of institutional practices spanning three centuries of denied equal opportunities, being discriminated against and deprived of basic human rights. Gibbs noted that double standards have been applied in a blatantly hypocritical manner to attribute immoral and deviant motives to these young adults while the same type of behavior by white youth is tolerated, excused, ignored, and/or exonerated.

Facing such adversity, it is little wonder that many low-income inner-city African-American male adolescents experience great difficulty making a transition to independent living. This case study was developed to better understand the institutional factors that may impede the efforts of four selected low-income juvenile court African-American adolescents to reach independent lifestyles. The study was designed to permit these individuals to practice independent living from a practical frame of reference examining daily living requirements. Additionally, the study allowed the participants to describe their experiences from entry through six months to the conclusion of the case study. The researcher is hopeful that capturing the experiences of the participants during the case study will reveal the types of institutional factors that impact these four participants as they attempt to make a transition to independent living lifestyles. Results of this study may lead to greater insight into the relationship between adverse institution factors and African-American male adolescents' efforts to reach independent lifestyles. In addition, the researcher believes that the case study findings will reveal the types of supportive community services needed to decrease the impact of adverse institutional factors on these four participants as they attempt to reach an increased level of self-reliance. Further, this study may inspire decision makers at the federal, state, and local levels to consider increased funding in support of independent living programs for African-American male adolescents.

RESEARCHER'S PAST PERSONAL AND PROFESSIONAL EXPERIENCES

As a parent of two African-American males, this researcher personally experienced difficulties rearing children in an urban environment. These experiences were personal testimony to how institutional factors impacted this population. Their testimony further illustrated the need for this case study.

5

From their early adolescent years through their current ages of 26 and 31, the researcher watched both biological sons struggle towards obtaining independent living status. The researcher personally felt a great deal of stress as she observed them struggle in their attempts to secure gainful employment, adequate housing, and health care services. While they frequented the recreational center located near their home, their primary source of cultural and social enjoyment came from within their family environment. Both of the researcher's biological sons had to guard themselves against getting caught up in the legal system. For example, during her older son's early teenage years, he was once chased at gunpoint by three undercover white police officers who suspected he was trying to break into the home of one of his friends, who lived on the next block. The undercover police officers were strangers to him. They could not be identified as police officers because they were in an unmarked car. They were not in uniform, and they were white men in a community that was primarily made up of African-Americans. When these men approached her son, he became frightened and ran for his life. But, he was not able to escape them and as a result, he was caught by the police officers and taken to the police station, fingerprinted and jailed. Fortunately, after the police officers decided that their suspicion of him was incorrect, they called his home to inform his mother that her son was at the police station and that he could be picked up and brought home. The experience was traumatic for the researcher's son, but with support from his family, he overcame that experience.

Observations of the attempts of inner-city African-American male adolescents' efforts to reach independent living status have extended beyond the researcher's biological sons. For example, since January, 1991, five inner-city African-American males, ranging in age from 14 to 18 years old, have lived in the researcher's home as foster sons. One foster son was placed in her residence in January 1991. Since that time he has completed high school and enrolled in college. After two years under supervision of the researcher, he moved to an independent living status and has struggled to live an independent lifestyle. Two other foster sons who resided in her home were on respite status while their foster parents took vacations. Another resided in her home

6

as a foster son for three months, but had to be removed due to a conflict with the foster son who was placed in January, 1991. The fifth foster son began residing in her home since March 1993 and has returned to his family.

Similar to the researcher's personal experiences, her professional experiences also offered her opportunities to observe the problems of some members of this group. These experiences occurred during her employment with an agency funded through the local community mental health board. Experiences with that agency included assessment of the needs of emotionally impaired young adult males and females. Many of the clients were inner-city African-American males between the ages of 17 to 21 years old. Most were diagnosed as having emotional problems with more than half receiving prescribed psychotropic medication. Some of their social and economic problems included unemployment, high school dropout, juvenile delinquency, drug and alcohol abuse or drug trafficking. Adequate access to health care, educational and recreational services was limited. Many of these young adults were totally dependent on the welfare system for financial assistance, food stamps, Medicaid coverage and their overall well-being.

These kinds of problems faced by the researcher's biological sons, her foster sons, and the clients serviced by the community mental health agency inspired her to conduct research to determine the extent that institutional factors, such as unemployment, adverse educational opportunities, social injustice as well as other factors, have on African-American male adolescents' efforts to reach independent lifestyles. While the researcher recognized that many other ethnic groups may experience similar problems, she decided to focus on the group that the media portrays as having the greatest degree of problems and is considered by many researchers to be an endangered species.

Having had personal and professional experiences with some members of this group, the researcher found her quest was to design and implement a program that would make a difference in the lives of African-American male adolescents. To that end, the researcher designed a program that provided a means whereby these adolescents practiced independent living in addition to receiving support community services. Additionally, the researcher conducted a case study on these adolescents to gather data on their experiences.

With the information presented in this chapter, the researcher believes that she has built a case demonstrating the strong social significance of the impact that institutional factors have on the struggle of African-American males' efforts to reach independent lifestyles. The researcher agreed with Senator Riegle's statement that as a nation we must find ways to change the directions of the trends of problems impacting this group of individuals.

Further, the researcher believes that this study will fill in gaps and offer greater insight into strategies useful in impacting institutional factors impeding African-American male adolescents' efforts to acquire self-sufficiency. The experiences of four African-American male adolescents provided data based on firsthand accounts of their struggles to reach independence.

The next chapter is a review of the literature pertinent to the institutional factors that impede African-American male adolescents' efforts to reach independent living lifestyles.

TWO

Review of the Literature

INTRODUCTION

During the past three years, this researcher conducted an intensive search to find research studies that were directly related to the research questions as indicated in chapter one. Sufficient empirical research studies had not yet been conducted related to these questions. None of the literature reviewed specifically focused on the research questions, although the researcher did find literature that focused on independent living skills training. The people previously studied included severely handicapped youth, individuals with mental retardation, blind and visually impaired adolescents, elderly persons with mental retardation, young adults with learning disabilities, as well as gifted children. Each of the mentioned populations had been labeled, with special services provided for independent living skills training. Since the researcher could not find similar literature on the research questions, the researcher decided to review literature on the institutional factors that impeded African-American male adolescents' efforts to reach independent lifestyles, whether labeled or not. During the literature search, the researcher found data on a variety of social and economic conditions that adversely impacted these adolescents. However, for the purpose of this study, only unemployment and unequal educational opportunities are included in this chapter.

A discussion of the research literature was separated into three sections. The first section is an overview of Child Welfare League of America (CWLA) findings and recommendations. The second section discusses employment opportunities (or the lack of) and their causes, consequences, and impact. The third section discusses unequal educational opportunities and their consequences.

SECTION ONE

Overview of Child Welfare League of America (CWLA) Standards for Independent Living Services

According to (CWLA) Standards for Independent Living Services (1989), acquiring self-sufficiency has been a struggle for adolescents in today's society, in general. However, for African-American adolescents, the struggle has been even greater as they not only must acquire the skills needed for normal development, but must also overcome the experience of personal and institutional racism. The CWLA cited that the struggle has been even greater for adolescents who leave home due to poor relationships with their family members or due to their own initiative. CWLA further reported that this group of adolescents has unique problems, such as family conflict, abuse or neglect, emotional problems, and social and economic constraints and that such problems have often impaired their ability to effectively advance. As a result they may need specialized services. As these youth did not receive the kinds of services needed to equip them with the skills to manage the responsibilities associated with adulthood, they became wards of the state and relied heavily on the state system rather than their families to provide care and supervision to them.

The CWLA pointed out that within the past few years, the population of children for whom the state was responsible for providing supervision had shifted substantially from younger to older. These children were often placed with agencies that are part of the foster care system. D. Gray (1991) puts the number of African-American males in foster care at 67 percent of the foster care enrollment for 1989. A report from the State of Michigan Department of Social Services (currently the Family Independent Agency) Wayne County Child Foster Care System

10

Administration Zone Office (1992) indicated that the number of children in foster care was 10,797 out of home placement, 78 percent of that number being African-American children. The report did not indicate the percentage of African-American young males in these numbers. The CWLA reported that with this increase, the need for service providers to service adolescents has become more severe. The agency indicated that unfortunately, many service providers have not established policies and procedures designed to create a structure whereby programs can teach independent living skills to adolescents upon entry into the agency.

Further, the CWLA reported that it is likely that some of the most serious barriers to assisting these children in advancing towards independence were restrictions in law and policy that required service providers to abruptly terminate their services to adolescents at specific ages. The CWLA cited that in some areas in North America, federal support for programs that provided independent living services was age limited. As a result, it has been difficult for agencies to provide such services to youth who are eighteen years old and are high school graduates, or who are eighteen but have not yet completed high school.

The CWLA had other concerns about service for adolescents. They reported that not only are age limits for terminating agency support often untimely and abrupt, but the range of service options allowed by state law and policy are often extremely narrow and limited. Additionally, agencies are usually prevented from obtaining resources needed to provide financial assistance, guidance or directions after an adolescent has reached the age-range restriction. As a result, these adolescents move from highly structured supervision and primary financial dependency to a situation that leaves them without intensive supervision, as well as without financial assistance.

CWLA suggested that, to become better service providers to these older children, it is the responsibility of child welfare agencies to develop policies and procedures, and programs geared towards teaching independent living skills as a primary goal.

11

SECTION TWO

Unemployment as an Adverse Institutional Factor

According to a report published by the U.S. Government Printing Office entitled: *The Plight of African-American Men In Urban America* (1991), Senator Donald Riegle discussed his concern about the scope of the problems young black men face in American society. He stated that a convergence of historic and current forces, including discrimination in employment opportunities, impeded the inclusion of African-American men in the mainstream of America. He reported that unemployment and earning gaps between college-graduate African-American men and white men was greater in 1990 than it was ten years earlier. Additionally, that income and employment disparities resulted in decreased access to credit for housing and for small business development. Senator Riegle went on to say that *"Poverty and slums and almost all of the ills of America are tied up, somehow, with the status of black men."* (P.2.)

Similarly, many social science researchers have also reported their concerns about employment issues impacting African-American male adolescents. Their discussion on these issues is cited in the following paragraphs. Researchers Gibbs (1988); Kunjufu (1989); Jones (1989) and Gray (1991), reported that in general, African-American male adolescents' economic status is disproportionately lower than their white counterparts. More specifically, in 1990, according to Gray (1991), African-American males in the State of Michigan had an unemployment rate of 17.9 compared to 6.8 percent for white males. He stated further that in 1990, the unemployment rate for the Metropolitan Detroit Statistical Areas, including the seven surrounding counties of Wayne, Monroe, Livingston, Oakland, Macomb, Lapeer, and St. Clair was 19.2 percent for African-American males compared to 6.8 for white males. Gray further reported that in the city of Detroit in 1990, the rate of unemployment for African-American males was 21.3 percent versus 10.6 percent for white males. The unemployment rate for these adolescents seemed to worsen, for example, according to the *Black News Digest*, in January of 1992, when unemployment for these adolescents was 29.0 percent.

For these researchers, high unemployment rates among African-American male adolescents are equated with conditions that breed poverty. One of the conditions the researchers believe creates poverty among these adolescents is having grown up in households of single mothers whose financial status was at poverty level. C. E. Bennett (1991) observed that the poverty rate for African-American families with female single-headed household without a spouse present has varied widely within the past twenty years. He also observed that "the poverty rate ranged from 46.5 percent in 1978 to 61.6 percent in 1989." Additionally, he stated that, in 1989, 4.3 million or 43.2 percent of all black-related children and 7.2 million or 14.1 percent of all white-related children under eighteen years of age lived with families who were poor (p. 16). Figures indicating the number of children living in poverty for the year of 1992 were different from the year of 1989. For example, according to a report written in the *Statistical Abstract of the United States* (1994) in the year of 1992, the number of children under the age of eighteen years old living with poor families was 2.3 million or 65.3 percent black children and 2.8 million or 17.6 percent of white children. As indicated in the above-mentioned figures, the number of children living in poverty remains high. Thus, it continues to pose a major problem for the survival of children in this country.

Causes of Unemployment

Such facts alone, as presented in the above discussion, have not been sufficient to help social scientists understand the scope of the problems faced by African-American male adolescents today. In order to advocate with any success for changes in the systematic institutional factors contributing to unemployment among these adolescents, one must first understand some causes of unemployment. In this way it is likely that one can identify the core of the problem and can better develop and implement strategies designed to eradicate this critical problem of unemployment.

According to T. Duster (1987), in many cities a rise in unemployment among a disproportionate number of African-American male adolescents resulted in part from the decline in the availability of manufacturing jobs and a rise in low-pay and no-benefit service kinds of employment opportunities. Duster suggested that unemployment resulted from immigration patterns, competition among many adolescent groups, and advances in technology. Others addressing the causes included Akbar (1992), Oliver (1989), Hill (1992), and Wilson (1991), who argue that unemployment among these adolescents was racially motivated. They suspected that many of these adolescents are discriminated against by many employers, particularly those employers who are members of the white society and covertly believe that African-Americans are inherently inferior and would not/could not perform to expected standards. Others suspect they are fearful of the loss of jobs for whites. The researchers conclude that, while the African-American male adolescents have had no direct control over influencing powerful institutional practices, they nevertheless have been victims of the consequences of unemployment. They were the ones most adversely impacted by unemployment and also the ones who suffered most as a result of the consequences of unemployment.

Consequences of Unemployment

Some researchers assert that there are several consequences that result from unemployment and underemployment. According to Chiricos and Bales (1991) and MacCoun and Reuter (1992), many African-American unemployed and underemployed were forced into alternative means of securing financial resources, ones that are often illegal. They report in a study of drug dealers, conducted in Washington, D.C., that there were approximately 14,544 different adults charged with drug distribution from 1985 to 1987. Seventy-nine percent of those charged were District residents; of these, 88 percent were males, 40 percent were between the ages of 18 to 24 years and 99 percent were African-Americans. Further, the researchers report that an estimated of one out of six African-American males between the ages of 17 to 20 years during the three-year period were charged with drug trafficking.

14

In Michigan the incarceration rate of these adolescents was also high. For example, according to articles written in the *Detroit Free Press* (1992) and (1994), during the years of 1980–1993, the Michigan prison population grew from 12,999 to 36,368. The report further indicated that in 1993, drug offenders made up 30 percent of all recent inmates compared to 7 percent in 1992. The article did not indicate, however, the percentage of African-American male adolescents included in the prison population. D. Gray (1991) reported that in 1990, African-American men made up 57.6 percent of the Michigan prison population. Additionally, 55 percent were on parole and 71 percent were juvenile detainees. Kenneth McGinnis, Michigan Correctional Director, expressed concern about the imprisonment rate in Michigan. According to a report written in the *Detroit Free Press* (1992), McGinnis stated that, "The state prison system is descending into a crisis that can be solved only if government officials find the courage to stop keeping so many people behind bars" (p.3A). McGinnis went on to discuss the need to have adequate financial resources for education and mental health services designed to help decrease entry into the prison system. But, instead of government officials moving to decrease the prison population, seemingly, they are preparing the means to house more prisoners.

This is evident in Congress's decision to increase the spending of money to build additional prisons. According to the *Congressional Record, Proceedings and Debates of the 103rd Congress, Second Session* (1994), the Revised Crime Bill, PA8819, allocated $7.9 billion for grants to states to construct new prisons. State spending for prisons has already exceeded state spending for education in local and intermediate districts. The *Detroit Free Press* (December 23, 1992) reported projected spending for corrections in 1993, for the State of Michigan, was expected to be approximately $1 billion; as much as 10 percent more than for the year of 1992.

On the other hand, the spending for education in the Michigan Public Schools was much less than that for correction facilities. This can be seen in a report written for the Michigan State Board of Education, "Conditions of Michigan Education" (1992). The report indicated that the total state aid, which includes the general membership aid from the state government to public schools, was $2,376 million. The membership included local and intermediate school districts in Michigan between the years of 1990–1991. The report did not included projected spending for the years of 1992–1993.

The last statement brings us to the point of discussing another institutional factor some researchers believe has an impact on these adolescents' efforts to reach independent living status. This institutional factor is unequal educational opportunities. A discussion of these challenges is included in Section Three.

SECTION THREE

Unequal Educational Opportunities

In reviewing the literature, this researcher found that there was a great amount of data on adverse unequal educational factors impacting the African-American male adolescent student, but only three that are directly related to this study are discussed in this section. They include suspension, high school dropout, and tracking or ability grouping.

D. Gray (1991) conducted research on the suspension of African-American male students in the City of Detroit and found that from 1989–1990 suspension of these adolescents from Detroit Public Schools comprised 66.4 percent. However, this population made up only 39 percent of the Detroit Public School student graduates. Additionally, Gray reported that in the 1989–1990 school years, the percent of African-American male students who dropped out of school was 54 percent.

R. J. Jones (1989) asserted that inadequate education made certain these adolescents would not have the basic certificate needed in American society for obtaining entry-level jobs, entering colleges, the armed forces, or apprenticeship programs. This would leave these adolescents at a disadvantage in attaining independent lifestyles.

The third unequal educational opportunity is tracking or ability grouping practices. This was defined by J. Kunjufu (1984)

16

as advance placement of honor students, mainstreaming regular students, or placement of students in low tracks, such as special education classes. Low tracking was considered by some researchers to be an adverse educational experience for many African-American male students. According to Brodbelt (1991) and Kunjufu (1989), a disproportionate number of these adolescent male students were slotted in special education classes. According to a report from the Detroit Public School "Student Counts by Race and Sex" (1992), in Detroit, Michigan, for the year of 1992, a disproportionate number of African-American male students were placed in special education classes. For example 6,672 African-American male students, as opposed to 615 white males, were placed in special education classes. Manning and Lucking (1990), asserted that the best method of grouping students for learning experiences has been an issue for many decades.

Nevertheless, S. Brodbelt (1991) contends that public schools have often tracked African-American students in substandard classrooms. F. E. Obiakor (1992) argued that, despite efforts made by legal and legislative systems to prevent tracking or ability grouping, such practices continued to exist in many public schools. Facing such critical issues, the need for solution appears to present the opportunity for social workers, working in conjunction with other professionals, politicians, community leaders, and parents, to advocate for educational reform. G. A. Smith (1992) stated that this issue must be demonstrated to policy makers, in conjunction with the idea that schools designed to provide challenging, yet supportive environments can successfully lead to increased rates of student participation and retention.

Smith also reported that magnet schools and schools of choice are new approaches to restructuring traditional academic practices. These schools were supposedly designed to enhance students' chances to obtain an adequate education. Based upon the social, economic and political thinking espoused by those who impact societal values, one would think that obtaining an education would assure gainful employment. However, Senator Riegle reported that African-American male engineers are unemployed at three times the rate of white engineers. He, as well as J. R. Meisenheimer II (1990), indicated that the higher the educational level, the bleaker the employment opportunities are for African-American males as opposed to white males. M. E. Thomas (1993), while testing the scope of class and race, found that African-Americans with higher levels of education and occupational class experienced more disadvantages than lower class African-Americans when compared to their white counterparts. Thus, discrimination against African-Americans across class lines apparently continues to exist.

Consequences of Tracking or Ability Grouping

The practice of tracking, according to S. Brodbelt (1991), restricted educational opportunities because labeling had all sorts of consequences, including the loss of self-confidence and self-respect. Those in low track placements were less likely to achieve social skills and experience a variety of curricular participation. Leake and Leake (1992) and P. Kean (1993) reported that tracking practices might result in many African-American students being under-educated. P. S. George (1992) suggested that tracking practices may limit many educators' perceptions of the need to support the student's efforts to establish a sense of self-esteem. The implication of tracking, according to George (1992), was that students were expected to acquire knowledge at different levels of degree.

A discussion of these critical problems brings us to the essence of this research case study. This case study project was designed to investigate the experiences of four low-income, state juvenile court ward, urban African-American male adolescents as they practiced independent living lifestyles while receiving supportive community services from Don Bosco Hall. This research was intended to fill the gap in the researcher's questions by providing data on the first-hand experiences of these four participants, who were impacted by institutional factors as they attempted to reach a greater level of independence than when they first entered the case study. This research study continues with chapter three, entitled, "Research Model: Case Study Research Design and Methodology."

THREE

Research Model: Case Study Research Design and Methodology

This chapter contains the study proposition, methodology, assumption, methods of data analysis, descriptive approach, and procedures. Additionally, data collection methods, instruments, an introduction to Don Bosco Hall, and an introduction to the Supervised Practice Independent Living Skills Training (SPILST) living quarters are included.

According to R. K. Yin (1989), the case study model is considered as weak and lacking sufficient precision, vigor, and objectivity. The model is often used by many disciplines and fields, such as anthropology, sociology, political science, psychology, management science, public administration, economics, public policy, education, and history. Yin went on to say, "a case study is an empirical inquiry when it investigates a contemporary phenomenon with its real-life context, when the boundaries between phenomenon and context are not clearly evident, and when multiple sources of evidence are used" (p.23). He concluded that case study research is a non-laboratory social science model, which permits naturalistic observation and interviews. In addition the model permits case histories as sources of data. For these reasons, the case study model was chosen for this investigation.

Application Important to Case Study

Yin noted four different applications important to conducting a case study. One application is to explain causal links in the real-life interventions that are too complex for the survey or experimental strategies. Another application describes the real-life context in which an intervention has occurred. The third application is a descriptive mode, from an illustrative case study of the intervention itself. The fourth application may be used to explore those situations in which the intervention being evaluated has no clear, single set of outcomes" (p. 25).

In this case study, the researcher used the descriptive mode application. To that end, the researcher presented case study illustrations to describe each of the participants' experiences over a six-month period of time.

Conditions Related to Research Strategies

Yin discussed three conditions to be considered when conducting research studies. They were (1) the form of the research question posed (i.e., "how," "why" questions); (2) the extent of control the researcher has over the actual behavioral events of the participants; and (3) whether the focus of the study was on historical as opposed to contemporary events. In this case study two of the three conditions were important. The first was the "how" form of question. The researcher wanted to know how each study proposition impacted the young men's efforts to reach independent living lifestyles. In the second condition, the researcher described the contemporary events that occurred in the lives of the participants.

Components Important to the Research Design

Yin listed five components especially important to the case study research design: (1) A study's question; (2) its propositions, if any; (3) its units(s) of analysis; (4) the logic linking the data to the propositions; and (5) the criteria for interpreting the findings.

According to Yin, there are five basic forms of questions: "who," "what," "where," "how," and "why." Certain types of questions favor certain types of research strategies. For example, "how" and "why" questions would favor experiment, history, and a case study strategy. On the other hand, "who," "what," "where," "how many," and "how much" favor survey and archival analysis strategies. In this case study, the researcher used the "how" question.

Yin stated that the study propositions direct attention to something that is to be examined within the scope of the study. In this case study, the researcher identified four propositions helpful to focusing on the relevant information about the participants.

Yin contended that the unit of analysis relates to the case to be studied. In this instance the African-American male adolescents' experiences as they practiced independent living were the primary unit of analysis.

Yin asserted that linking data to propositions may be accomplished by pattern matching. In this instance, pattern matching was accomplished by matching data collected through interviews with the young men to the case study propositions.

Criteria for interpreting the study's findings are most difficult to achieve, Yin states. In this case study, the researcher reviewed relevant literature to find criteria that defined adverse unemployment as well as unequal educational opportunities. Additionally, the researcher attempted to match the pattern of experiences of the participants to the identified criteria.

A. STUDY PROPOSITION

The case study propositions were that (1) Adverse institutional factors, such as unemployment and unequal educational opportunities, impede African-American adolescents' efforts to reach independent lifestyles; (2) Supervised practiced independent living skills training can improve independent living skills among low-income, state court-ward urban African-American male adolescents; (3) Public supportive community services can assist in the achievement of independent living skills of these youth and; (4) Advocacy techniques conducted by supportive community agencies on the behalf of African-American male adolescents can decrease the adverse impact that institutional factors have on their efforts to achieve independent living lifestyles.

B. ASSUMPTION

The researcher assumed that, if the presence of institutional factors such as unemployment and unequal educational opportunities impeded these adolescents' efforts to gain independence, then the provision of supportive and advocacy services to help them deal with discrimination could increase their chances to gain independent lifestyles. From this assumption came the development of the Supervised Practice Independent Living Skills Training (SPILST) Program living quarters designed for the participants in the case study.

C. METHODOLOGY

Participants

The participants were four low-income, urban African-American male youth, 18 to 20 years old. They were temporary Juvenile Court wards of the State of Michigan because of foster care response to abuse and neglect petitions. The method by which they became wards of the court was through the Michigan Department of Social Services' petitioning of the court to take temporary custody of them away from their biological parents. This petitioning occurred because of allegations or facts of behavioral at-risk conditions and/or conditions of harm while living in their immediate environment.

In these instances, legal custody was taken from the legal guardian. These four participants allegedly experienced such conditions prior to being placed at Don Bosco Hall, an alternative residential facility for state wards. The court assigned them to the Michigan Department of Social Services (MDSS). MDSS placed them with a community agency, and that agency provided support and supervision. In this instance, Don Bosco Hall was assigned as the legal service provider for these adolescents. Their wardship began at an early age and continued through conclusion of the case study. They all received supportive community services from Don Bosco Hall during the duration of the case study.

Selection of Participants

The participants were identified and selected to participate in the study by the Director of the Supervised Independent Living Program, the Supervisor of Transitional Living Program Services, and Case Managers at Don Bosco Hall. Those participants selected were considered to pose the least liability to Don Bosco Hall and the home owner of the SPILST Program living quarters. As a result, this kind of selection may have biased the participants and/or the study.

Criteria for Selection

The participants were carefully selected based on the following criteria:

1. Their willingness to function at least moderately in a group setting with moderate to minimum supervision required.
2. Their willingness to cooperate at least moderately with authority figures.
3. Their agreement to follow rules and regulations, which included no drinking, using drugs, carrying an illegal weapon, or loitering around their living quarters.
4. Their expressed interest in practicing independent living functioning.
5. Their expressed interest in continuing to receive supportive community services from Don Bosco Hall while practicing independent living skills within the context of the (SPILST) Program living quarters.
6. They would be eighteen years old by the date of placement into the SPILST Program living quarters. However, they could not reach age twenty-one before the end of the case study.
7. Their behavior demonstrated that they were not dangerous to themselves or others.
8. They were wards of the Michigan juvenile court system.

9. They signed a consent agreement to participate in the case study.
10. They expressed interest in seeking, securing and maintaining employment or attending school.

Personal and Family History of Participants

During the interview process, these participants described their personal and family history while responding to an oral questionnaire. The data were gathered to get a cogent picture of their personal and family psycho-social backgrounds.

Payment for Participation

The participants were paid a one-time-only sum of fifteen dollars each by the researcher for their participation in the case study.

Confidentiality and Protection of Identity of Participants

To protect the identity of the participants, their real names were not used. Rather, they were given identification numbers and assumed names. However, their real names appeared on the consent forms acknowledging participation. Such forms were kept in a safe place, only to be seen by the researcher and Don Bosco Hall's employees, management staff members, and the administrator.

Generalization/Limitations

This was a descriptive case study that would need to be tested with a larger number of African-American male adolescent participants in order to be generalized. The case study was limited to four African-American male adolescents ages 18 to 21 years. These participants are citizens of the Detroit, Michigan, area only. These factors, limited the possibility of generalizing these findings to all adolescents.

D. METHOD OF DATA ANALYSIS—DESCRIPTIVE APPROACH

The descriptive approach was used to describe the participants' independent living experiences during the case study. Since the descriptive mode was used, causal inferences were not possible.

Chronological Structure

In Yin's (1989) model, the dominant model of analysis was use of chronologies—a special form of time series. This mode of analysis allowed the researcher to trace the participants' experiences over time and to present the evidence in chronological order. The indicators traced over time were: 1) barriers to independent living and how Don Bosco Hall services impacted barriers faced by these participants, and 2) the participants' level of independent living functioning from entry level to three and six months after their participation in the case study.

The Lesser Mode of Analysis

The lesser mode of analysis was the opinion of the Supervisor of Transitional Living Program at Don Bosco Hall. His observations were used to form his opinions about the participants' level of independent functioning at entry level and three and six months after their participation in the case study.

A narrative written form was used to describe and analyze the cases involved in the case study. Written analysis is included in chapter four, under the title: "Management and Analysis of the Data."

E. PROCEDURES

Prior to initiating the case study procedures, several meetings were conducted with the Executive Director of Don Bosco Hall, the Director of Supervised Independent Living Program, and the Supervisor of Transitional Living Program at Don Bosco Hall. During these meetings the researcher explained the philosophy, goals, and objectives of the study. Upon expressing an interest in participating in the case study, representatives of Don Bosco Hall signed an agreement to participate. In addition, they agreed to explain the case study to their clients and to inquire about their interest in participating.

After Don Bosco Hall explained the case study to the clients, several of them offered to participate. Four were selected by Don Bosco Hall to participate in the case study. During the initial meeting, the participants were informed by the researcher about the confidentiality issues, withdrawal procedures, home rules and regulations, and informed consent procedures. At that meeting they signed a consent to participate and a rental agreement in order to begin the practical activities. The case study began in March of 1993.

F. DATA COLLECTION METHODS

The data was collected using three separate face-to-face interviews with each of the four participants. Interview settings were chosen depending on the participants' needs. For their convenience, interviews were conducted on the premises of the living quarters or other settings, as appropriate.

Entry Level Interviews

The first face-to-face interviews were completed with each of the four participants within the first week of placement into the Supervised Practice Independent Living Skills Training (SPILST) Program living quarters. The interviews were conducted on the premises of the SPILST Program living quarters. The first interviews were twofold:

1. To gather data about their personal and family history using the "Psycho-social History Assessment" questionnaire.
2. To gather data about their level of independent living experiences at entry level into the case study. The instrument used was the Supervised Practice Independent Living Skills Training tool.

Second Interview

The second face-to-face interviews were completed within three months of the participants' participation in the case study. Three of the participants were interviewed on the premises of the SPILST Program living quarters. The fourth participant was involved in an illegal activity and arrested by the police, resulting in his being removed from the independent living quarters and returned to Don Bosco Hall's on-site residential facilities. Therefore, the second interview session with this participant was conducted later on the premises of Don Bosco Hall.

Third Interview

The third face-to-face interviews were conducted within six months of these young mens' participation in the case study. The two participants who continued to reside in the independent living quarters were interviewed in their living quarters. At the time of the third interview, one of the participants had enrolled in a college outside of Detroit. On his return home, he was interviewed in the home of his godparents. Due to the other participant's continued stay on the premises of Don Bosco Hall, he was again interviewed on those premises.

Interview with Don Bosco Hall Representative

Three face-to-face interviews were conducted at Don Bosco Hall with the Supervisor of the Transitional Living Program.

The instrument used was an "Open Ended Questionnaire." All interviews with the participants and the supervisor were cassette taped and were transcribed within two weeks of the date of the interviews. Hard copies of the transcribed data were kept as a source of raw data and used to report the findings of the study.

G. INSTRUMENTS

All instruments were developed and administered by the researcher. The first instrument was the "Psycho-social History Assessment" questionnaire. The instrument was used as a method to gather data about participants' personal and family history. Questions were asked about: (a) Statement of problems, parental, siblings, and extended family members; (b) Their own developmental history, socialization, behavioral, vocational and legal experiences; (c) The researcher's impression of the participants' insight and judgment, level of independence, socialization and educational skills, and (d) Their attitude and behavior.

The second instrument used was the "Supervised Practice Independent Living Skills Training Tool." This tool was also an open-ended questionnaire. The researcher administered the questionnaire to the four participants. This questionnaire consisted of nine different category items important to independent living functioning. The items included: (a) Housing, (b) Employment/unemployment, (c) Education, (d) Health care, (e) Crime and delinquency, (f) Socialization/social relationships, (g) Recreational activities, (h) Violence, and (i) Transportation. Within those category items was a total of eighty questions. The questions were used to gather data about the participants' experiences at entry level and within three and six months of their participation in the case study.

The third instrument was the open-ended version of the second questionnaire. It was administered to the Supervisor of Transitional Living Program at Don Bosco Hall. The questionnaire consisted of the same nine category items: (a) Housing, (b) Employment/unemployment, (c) Education, (d) Health care, (e) Crime and delinquency, (f) Socialization/social relationships, (g)

Recreational activities, (h) Violence, and (i) Transportation. Among those category items was a total of eighty-two questions. When answering these eighty-two questions, the representative gave his opinion about the participants' experiences at entry level and as they practiced living independently during their participation in the case study. He also described how the supportive community services assisted in the achievement of independent living skills of the participants.

H. BACKGROUND ON DON BOSCO HALL

Don Bosco Hall is a community-based treatment center that has provided services to children and adolescent males since 1954. It is licensed by the State of Michigan Department of Social Services and is a constituent agency of the Archdiocese of Detroit, Michigan. The agency provides an array of services that includes: workshops, individual counseling, case management, respite, semi-independent living, and residential services. The services are provided to youth by a network of qualified professional individuals who work as a team to enhance the lives of youth. Referrals to Don Bosco Hall are accepted from private agencies, Probate Court, and the Department of Social Services.

I. INTRODUCTION TO THE SUPERVISED PRACTICE INDEPENDENT LIVING SKILLS TRAINING (SPILST) PROGRAM LIVING QUARTERS

The SPILST Program was conceptualized in August of 1992, and became operational in 1993, for this case study. The researcher/renter designed this program to create an opportunity for adolescents to learn from a practical frame of reference, independent living skills. The (SPILST) Program living quarters provided a stable and least restrictive community living arrangement for these adolescents. In this study they were allowed to try and fail and try again to gain the highest level of independent living skills possible during these six months of the case study. To begin the practical living arrangement and to set boundaries for living in the SPILST Program, the participants signed a rental agreement.

Rules and Regulations of the Rental Agreement

The signed rental agreement between the participants and their landlord/researcher included rules and regulations that governed the landlord-renter relationship. Breach of these rules and regulations by the participants could result in termination of use of the living quarters. The rules and regulations were as follows:

1. The renter was not to have loud music, parties, fights, or events that would disturb the other residents at the living quarters.
2. Windows and doors were to be kept secure at all times.
3. The renter was not allowed to have high density traffic in and out of the premises.
4. The renter was not allowed to loiter on or around the premises.
5. The renter was to keep a clean and orderly apartment.
6. The renter was to attend high school on a regular and consistent basis.
7. The renter was to be involved in a work activity program.
8. The renter was to maintain contact with his community support agency as needed.
9. The renter (or anyone else) was not to have on the premises any illegal substances, including drugs or alcohol.
10. The renter was not to bring or allow anyone else to bring firearms on the premises.
11. The renter was not to intrude on the privacy of any person residing on the premises.

SPILST Program Philosophy to Service Provision

The philosophy was that all adolescents have a right to become empowered by learning skills to help them gain the highest level of independent living skills. In addition, that these adolescents receive the benefits and privileges granted to them as human beings and by law.

Goals

The goals of the SPILST Program were to:

1. Provide a stable and least restrictive community living arrangement for adolescents between the ages of 18 and 21 years who required moderate to minimum supervision.
2. Provide services to adolescents to help them to acquire independent functioning skills useful in managing daily responsibilities, events, and intrinsic as well as extrinsic factors impacting their lives.

Objectives

Objectives of the SPILST Program for adolescents were to:

1. Increase self-reliance and self-advocacy skill.
2. Increase accessibility and opportunities for adequate educational and employment opportunities, and to manage educational and employment responsibilities.
3. Decrease risks for involvement in criminal, legal, and juvenile justice systems.
4. Increase financial security and decrease or eliminate dependency on public welfare systems.
5. Provide stable living conditions and establish or enhance home management skills functioning and increase health maintenance and health care.
6. Increase socialization/social relationships and involvement in recreational activities.

7. Increase accessibility and use of public or other modes of transportation.
8. Recognize degrees of success of independent functioning.
9. Establish positive norms, set limits, and follow rules and regulations.
10. Manage conflict, problem solve, and decrease exposure to violence.
11. Increase ability to set realistic short- and long-term goals, objectives, and expectations.
12. Increase ability to manage personal and adverse institutional challenges.

Training Methods

As a practice activity, training methods were used to meet the goals and objectives of the SPILST Program. They were conceptual in nature and were provided on face-to-face contacts. These training methods are outlined in numbers 1 through 3 as follows:

1. Workshop, which provided training in effective communication, conflict management, problem resolution, budgeting and time management.
2. Role plays, which included training in self-control and self-advocacy skills and effective use of strategies for negotiating with others.
3. Individual and group counseling around self-respect, self-esteem, health care, exercise, and basic diet issues.

Various methods were practical in nature and were most often provided through face-to-face contacts. Telephone contacts were sometimes used as a communication method as well. These practical methods are outlined in numbers 1 through 5 listed below:

1. In-home individual and group practice activities through assisting, directing, and/or guiding adolescents in their efforts to achieve independent living functioning.

2. Establishment of relationships with potential employers and making of job referrals and job placements.
3. Accompanying adolescents during employment interviews, meeting with school officials, police officers, juvenile justice system, and other agency officials when needed.
4. Provision of supervision through scheduled or unscheduled home visit and/or 24-hour telephone availability.
5. SPILST Program home providers and Don Bosco Hall professional collaborative efforts.

Category Items and Practical Methods

The SPILST Program identified nine category items and various practical methods important to independent living lifestyle. They were as follows:

a. Housing Category

Practical methods related to housing included the following activities: (1) participation in home management and operations, (2) house cleaning, (3) making minor household repairs and lawn-care maintenance, (4) health and fire safety rules, (5) efficient use of utilities, telephone, and appliances, (6) negotiating with landlord, utility, and telephone companies, (7) management of conflict among peers and visitors, (8) managing loneliness, (9) securing medical and dental services, (10) behaving towards peers and neighbors in a respectful and cooperative manner.

b. Employment Category

Practice methods related to securing and maintaining employment included (1) effective communication, using appropriate verbal expression, body language, and eye contact with potential and/or current employers, (2) completing résumés and job applications and being accessible and available for employment opportunities, (3) negotiating with employers for salaries, dressing appropriately, getting to work on time, and fulfilling employment obligations, and (4) complying with employment safety and regulations and maintaining good work habits.

c. Education Category

Increased awareness and practice techniques to maximize opportunities to remain in school and attain an adequate education were as follows: (1) getting to school on time, completing classroom and homework assignments, (2) turning in assignments on time, practicing study habits and skills needed to get along well with teachers and peers.

d. Health Category

Maintaining a good diet and exercise program, having knowledge and making adequate use of health-care resources were important. Additionally, early detection of health problems and follow-through with doctors' recommendations were important to this curriculum. Further, practicing safe sex methods and avoidance of alcohol and drug use were also important.

e. Crime and Delinquency Category

Factors identified as important were: (1) acquiring management and advocacy skills useful for managing extrinsic factors that may lead to involvement in the criminal and delinquent systems, (2) awareness of and ability to secure adequate legal services, (3) avoidance of possession of firearms, and (4) learning appropriate communication skills when responding to police officers and security guards and, when wrongfully being accused of involvement in criminal or violent activities.

f. Socialization/Social Relationships

Useful skills included: practice techniques helpful in establishing, reestablishing, or maintaining social relationships with same sex, opposite sex, and particularly peers. Additionally, making effective and efficient use of leisure time were important techniques.

g. Recreational Activities

Acquiring awareness of location of recreational facilities nearest living quarters, and being aware of hours of operation and services offered was an important skill.

h. Violence

Appropriate management of individual difficulties and environmental factors that might have increased the risk of involvement in the criminal justice system were important. Also, establishing or reestablishing appropriate problem-solving and conflict management and resolution skills were useful as well.

34

i. Transportation

Acquiring necessary resources to travel to and from destinations were important to this curriculum. In addition, awareness of public transportation routes and making arrangements for buddy/team transportation were included in this curriculum.

SPILST Setting

The setting for practice and the investigation of the case study was a residential home located in the inner-city of Detroit, Michigan, and the County of Wayne. The house had the image of a single dwelling, but it was made up of three separate units. These units were sectioned off into three different independent dwellings. The front door entrance led to a hallway. From this hallway, entry was available into the front door of the first-floor unit. This unit consisted of two bedrooms, a living room with fireplace, a kitchen, one bathroom, and several closet spaces.

Access to the second floor units could be made from a stairway, which led to the front doors of each of two units. Each of the second-floor units was made up of one bedroom, a living room, bathroom, a kitchen, and a number of closet spaces. Entrance and exit to both of the second-floor units was available via a stairway built on the back of the dwelling. The dwelling was located near main transportation bus lines and a main expressway. These living quarters were very important to the adolescents' opportunity to actually practice independent living skills. Although occupancy included four unrelated participants, a normal living arrangement was provided as much as possible.

Composition of Home Provider

The home provider was also the researcher.

Researchers' Desirable Qualities of the Home Provider

Desirable qualities of the home provider were important to these participants' opportunity to practice independent living. Desirable qualities were as follows:

1. Understanding and knowledge of the developmental stages of adolescents.
2. Making frequent and routine visits to review the home for upkeep and maintenance issues. Making home repairs as needed.
3. Sensitivity to the external institutional factors that may evoke feelings of anxiety and frustration within African-American male adolescents. Awareness that these feelings may be released through physical aggression against inanimate objects, such as the living quarters.
4. Understanding of and the willingness to facilitate the participants working through alternative expressions of aggression.
5. Sensitivity to the need for the African-American male participants to gain a sense of empowerment over their life experiences.
6. Supportive and affirming attitudes and behaviors toward the participants.
7. Ability to collaborate with the supportive community agency and other important systems.
8. Willingness and availability to provide telephone accessibility and to make home visits, if needed.
9. Willingness to act as extended family support and mediator to the participants.

Composition of Don Bosco Hall Staff that Provided Services to the Participants Was as Follows:

While not by design, the staff consisted of African-Americans, one female and three males, who were primarily responsible for providing in-home services to the participants. The staff ages ranged between 23 and 34 years old. Their professional degrees were bachelor level, with at least two years experience working with adolescent males.

Quality of Staff at Don Bosco Hall

Quality of the staff was significant to the case study. When interacting with the participants, the staff demonstrated such qualities as: (1) Tolerance, (2) Affirming attitude, (3) Listening and attentiveness, (4) Consistency, flexibility, and understanding, (5) Good advocacy skills.

Provision of Supportive Community Services

Don Bosco Hall was primarily responsible for providing services to the participants from both conceptual and practical forms of references. For example, from conceptual frames of references, services focused on concepts and values that guided behavior in the community, schools, employment, workshops, groups and individual counseling. From practical frames of references, these participants put into practice what they had learned from conceptual frames of references. Don Bosco Hall staff actively participated in hands-on, face-to-face daily living activities, such as budgeting, home and conflict management, problem-solving, securing employment, management of employment responsibilities, and transportation needs. Further, socialization, social relations, and health care were part of these services.

Don Bosco Hall staff often advocated on the participants' behalf when they were faced with environmental factors that impeded their progress towards independent living. They also monitored the activities of the participants as they guided, directed, taught, and supported them as they practiced living independently. There were generally two levels of monitoring provided by Don Bosco Hall. Level one was provided at both an intermediate and infrequent basis. Level two was provided on an increased frequency basis.

Level One: Intermediate and Infrequent Monitoring

During the first month of placement, intermediate and infrequent monitoring in the community was limited to only two to three scheduled home visits per week. Telephone contacts made throughout the day were also means of monitoring and giving verbal support, affirmation, and guidance to the participants. Surprise unscheduled home visits were made no more than three times per week. In general the participants were given a considerable amount of autonomy. They were allowed the opportunity to capitalize on their own intrinsic strength, as well as put into practice the knowledge and skills they acquired through conceptual and practical frames of references.

Level Two: Increased Frequency of Monitoring Provision

One and one half months after initial placement, the participants began to break many of the rules and regulations established for placement in the SPILST Program living quarters.

As a result of these rules being broken, it became apparent that the participants needed more intensive supervision. The staff at Don Bosco Hall, and the researcher/home provider met on several occasions to discuss such behavioral problems exhibited by the participants. These problems warranted increased monitoring in order to enhance the chances of the participants successfully reaching independent status and to decrease the liability to Don Bosco Hall and the researcher/home provider. The agreement established at these meetings was that Don Bosco Hall would increase the intensity and frequency of in-home visits with the participants. This allowed them time to increase their scheduled and unscheduled home visits to the participants' living quarters. During their scheduled visits, they would spend four hours per day, five days per week at the living quarters. Unscheduled in-home visits were increased from the three times per week to six to eight times per week.

Don Bosco Hall's staff increased their daily telephone calls to the home. In addition, the participants were required to telephone the staff immediately upon any signs of conflicts.

FOUR

Management and Analysis of the Data

These interviews were conducted with each participant at different times. Each of them told their stories about their personal and family experiences. Their real names were not used to protect their real identity.

BAYCO

This was the researcher's first interview with Bayco. This interview was conducted at the entry level of his participation in the SPILST Program living quarters. At this time questions were asked to obtain from him information about his personal history. The information is Bayco's opinion about his personal and family history.

Bayco described himself as being over six feet tall, eighteen years old, African-American male who weighed 180 to 190 pounds. He presented himself to be a happy-go-lucky young man, but as he told the researcher his life story, somewhat of an expression of sadness came over his face. Bayco began his story by stating that his parents divorced when he was three years old. He reported that after their divorce, his father left the home and he did not see his father again until he was twelve years old.

Bayco reported that his working mother alone raised him and his older brother and younger sister. He said that his relationship with his mother was meaningful until his younger sister was born. From that time on, he felt neglected by his mother because of the affection she gave to his sister. Bayco also stated that for a short period of time his brother attempted to assume the role of father. He said that when his brother stopped behaving in such a manner towards him, their relationship improved. Bayco said that when he was getting along poorly with his mother and brother, most of the time, he felt alone, without substantial emotional support from his family.

Bayco reported that during most of his high school years, his grade point average was about 3.5, but dropped to 1.4 by the time he reached the eleventh grade. He attributed this decline to a poor relationship with his mother. Bayco stated that he had a good relationship with his teachers and peers, but his comedian performance was often considered too much for his teachers to tolerate. Bayco said, "I like to tell jokes so I can make people laugh and make them happy. But I learned that the classroom was not the place to tell jokes."

Bayco stated that he was proud of himself because he could adapt to any situation that impacted his life. He said that he felt happy that he could repair cars and clean gutters. He stated that he felt pleased that he had not been involved in criminal activities. Also, he felt a sense of accomplishment in securing employment and having owned several used automobiles that he purchased with his own earnings.

Bayco reported that he was enrolled in the twelfth grade and was soon to graduate. He said that his plan was to enter college on a basketball scholarship immediately after graduation. Yet, despite his wishes for himself, Bayco continued to experience family difficulties that encouraged his running away from home. These circumstances resulted in his being placed in the Don Bosco Hall on site residential program. Bayco stated that he felt that his experience of being homeless for three weeks and living in Don Bosco Hall's Supervised Independent Living (SIL) program for approximately one year had prepared him to manage himself in the Supervised Practice Independent Living Skills Training (SPILST) Program independent living quarters. He reported that he believed that he could manage himself while practicing living in the SPILST Program living quarters. However, in the event he had any problems that he could not manage, he would seek assistance from the staff at Don Bosco Hall.

Interview with the Supervisor of the Transitional Living Program at Don Bosco Hall regarding Bayco

This was the first interview conducted with the Supervisor of the Transitional Living Program at Don Bosco Hall. He had these comments to make about Bayco: "At age seventeen, Bayco was homeless a few weeks before he came into the foster care system through the Michigan Department of Social Services. His involvement with that system occurred as a result of his being kicked out of his home by his mother. During these few weeks, he stayed a couple of weeks with the basketball coach who taught at the high school Bayco attended. But at the end of those few weeks, the coach turned him over to the Child Protective Services Division of the Michigan Department of Social Services. As he was seventeen years old, he was old enough to be placed in SIL program at Don Bosco Hall. It was alleged that he was kicked out of his home because his mother accused him of stealing from her. Although Bayco denied such accusations, it appeared that something was wrong between him and his mother.

"My assessment of this whole situation is that something had been going on. A mother does not kick out a child for allegedly stealing something. It had to have been something that was going on for a while. I am not saying that it was totally Bayco's fault, but it must have been a situation brewing for a while. I think that in this situation Bayco was failed by the system. Instead of Bayco's coming into Don Bosco Hall's SIL program, perhaps family support services should have been implemented. Perhaps, someone should have been going to the house three or four days a week to work with Bayco, his mother, and his siblings. If that had happened, he may still be at home today.

"I know that we, at Don Bosco Hall have tried, but I think now it is too late, since he's been living away from home. He has not really been having a cohesive relationship with his mother. Anytime we try to coordinate something with his mother and himself, his mother sabotages it, and does not want to participate. We hope that they can maintain a relationship that's beneficial to him. For example, he is going to college, perhaps she can support him in college. When a kid is in college, they still need things. The mother may send a meal up, send some money every now and then. We understand that the reality is he may not be able to stay at home, but she can still be supportive of him. In the meantime, I feel that Bayco is a good candidate for the SPILST Program living quarters. Based on many of his past experiences at Don Bosco, he will do well in the case study."

The researcher concluded from the interviews with the supervisor and Bayco that Bayco had some degree of independent living skills. He had employment skills and was consistent in maintaining his own transportation. He was motivated to complete high school and had realistic goals about going to college. Based on his demonstrated readiness to learn additional independent living skills, Bayco was selected by Don Bosco to participate in the case study. During the subsequent interview with Bayco, he seemed comfortable participating in the SPILST living program.

First Interview with Bayco

This was the first interview with Bayco at entry level into the SPILST Program. Bayco had not been responsible for seeking housing for himself nor having to pay his rent or pay his household expenses. Since he had been away from home and under the custody of the Juvenile Court System, the Michigan Department of Social Services (MDSS) had been responsible for providing financial services to meet such needs for Bayco. MDSS provided funding to Don Bosco Hall and that agency allocated funds to meet some of Bayco's needs. He expressed appreciation to Don Bosco Hall for securing the SPILST Program living quarters for him and paying his rent from the subsidy that he received from the Michigan Department of Social Services.

After signing an agreement to participate in the case study, he was placed into the two-bedroom apartment located on the first floor of the SPILST Program living quarters. In this living arrangement, he shared an apartment with one of the other participants also participating in the case study. For the first time in his life, he assumed responsibilities for home management and independent functioning. For example, Bayco used some of his allowance that he received from MDSS through Don

Bosco Hall and some of his earnings that he received from his employment to pay half of the utility and telephone bills. Bayco soon learned that he had to budget his money well so that it could last through the month. He usually kept his living quarters clean, so cleaning his apartment was not new to him.

Bayco felt that his house mate was often uncooperative and his house mate often left the responsibility of cleaning the living room and bathroom up to him. Bayco's personal habits were different from those of his house mate. For example, he did not like the radio to be turned up loud, but on the other hand, his house mate often turned the radio to full volume. Bayco felt that he needed quiet time after a day in school and after returning home from his part-time job. He was basically unhappy sharing the apartment with that particular house mate. He felt that they were entirely too different from each other to be able to share an apartment and work cooperatively as a team. Bayco felt that he needed a house mate who was more like himself, someone who was reserved and motivated to keep the apartment clean, hard working and scheduled quiet time to complete homework school assignments.

Second Interview with Bayco

The second interview was conducted three months after Bayco first began to participate in the case study. At the time of the second interview, Bayco was no longer living at the SPILST Program living quarters. At that time he had been arrested by the Detroit Police, as they found him carrying a sawed-off shot gun. He was jailed because of his criminal behavior, but after a couple of weeks, he was released to the custody of Don Bosco Hall. Because of his behavior, Bayco was not allowed to return to the SPILST Program. Instead he was returned to Don Bosco Hall's on-site Residential Program. As a result, the second interview with him was conducted on the premises of Don Bosco Hall.

Since Bayco was no longer practicing independent living skills in the context of the living quarters, he had limited information to share about the subject of independent living. When asked, he refused to discuss the incident that led to his being

43

arrested by the police. Additionally, he refused to discuss the allegations of his carrying an illegal weapon. Instead, Bayco wanted to talk about what he believed that the community could do to assist low-income urban African-American male adolescents obtain low-income housing and gainful employment.

The following are his comments: "I feel the community can assist inner city black males in seeking low-income housing; they can continue to do like what the community is already doing. They are opening their doors and letting us live with them as SIL residents. I hope that the community can help us with the future for ourselves in terms of employment opportunities."

Bayco went on to say, "I feel that a great number of African-American male adolescents have the hardest time securing employment because of the way that the City of Detroit views them. As well as because of racial discrimination practiced by some employers. I know that racial discrimination exists because I have experienced it in one way or another. Some of my peers have experienced it also. When it comes to getting a job, I have to really put forth an effort to enhance my chances of securing a job. When I look for a job, I dress in a suit, and express myself clearly and precisely. I explain to the potential employers that I am a young African-American man trying to earn money legally instead of getting into trouble. When I do get a job, I try very hard to maintain good work habits and prove myself to my employer. I feel that African-American male adolescents, more than any other groups, have to prove themselves to their employer."

Bayco went on to talk about employment problems for African-American male youth. "We don't even get a chance to get high technology jobs because we don't get the technological training like others do. We have to even have Don Bosco Hall to go on interviews with us to be an advocate on our behalf. What do you think about that?"

Bayco also discussed issues regarding low-income urban African-American young men's experiences while attending public school. He said that many African-American male adolescents have problems staying in school. He said that he was not sure of the reasons they dropped out of school. On second thought he said that some reasons may be that the class curriculum was not interesting enough for the students. He stated that having a teacher show that she cares about the student might be helpful in keeping students in school. Bayco said that the things that kept his interest in school were basketball, soccer, and other sports. In addition, he was liked by his peers and teachers.

Third Interview with Bayco

The third interview with Bayco was conducted six months after Bayco first entered the SPILST Program. The interview was conducted on the premises of Don Bosco Hall. During this interview Bayco again would not talk about the incident that led to his arrest. However, he finally admitted that one of the factors contributing to his involvement in a criminal activity was that he needed money to pay for some items that he needed. He stated that he did not have a job at the time, so he used other means to get his financial needs met. He also talked about the idea of using the gun to rob the rich and give the money to poor people. "One thing I have to tell you is that I never intended to get involved in any kind of criminal activity. I know that Don Bosco Hall and you counted on me to be a model for other young men. I have learned that, if a young man is involved in criminal activities, it will not help him at all. It might even mess up his life forever. The thing that I would say to young black men is, stay away from crime and learn to stand on your own two feet." Bayco stopped talking about the criminal activity and again explained his plans to attend college located out of the state of Michigan. He reported that he was proud of his academic accomplishments and was looking forward to playing college basketball. Bayco talked about his increased insight into the kinds of knowledge and skills needed to become an independently functioning individual in today's society. He stated that, even though his living arrangement in the SPILST Program living quarters was limited, he reported having learned to manage a home. He also reported being more aware of the qualities that he would like to have in a house mate when he is housed on a college campus.

Observation of the Supervisor of the Transitional Living Program at Don Bosco Hall

During the interview with the Supervisor of the Residential Program, he explained that this was Bayco's first time being arrested for criminal activities. The supervisor stated that Bayco admitted to carrying a gun but denied that he was in the process of car-jacking. He further stated that since this was Bayco's first arrest, he was given a second chance. The supervisor stated that one thing that motivated the police to release Bayco was that he was interested in going to college. Therefore, he was put on probation for two years and was allowed to leave Michigan to attend college. He states that Bayco could remain at college as long as he did not get involved in any other illegal activities.

The supervisor stated that Bayco had always been considered to be a good model for other residents. Therefore, Bayco's involvement in a criminal activity was certainly a shock to Don Bosco Hall's staff. He further stated that none of the staff would have ever suspected such behavior from Bayco. He reported that Bayco's behavior may have been attributed to being overwhelmed from the stress of struggling to reach independent living functioning. The supervisor went on to say, "One of the things that we did to help Bayco was to work with a university to help him to get accepted on a sports scholarship. One of the staff members at Don Bosco Hall had connections at the university. He made a few phone calls and got Bayco what he needed. I think that was great work that the staff person did."

Analysis by the Researcher

As is apparent, Bayco's stay at the SPILST Program living quarters was short lived due to his involvement in a criminal activity. The researcher considered Bayco to be one of the few fortunate African-American male adolescents in that he was not incarcerated but was released to Don Bosco Hall to receive guidance and supervision. With the assistance from Don Bosco Hall, Bayco even had a chance to enter college on a basketball scholarship. It is believed by the Supervisor of the Transitional Living

Program at Don Bosco Hall that his completion of college could be an asset and a means for him attaining independent functioning and self-sufficiency.

From the information obtained from Bayco, to the researcher it seemed as though an institutional factor such as unemployment influenced Bayco to behave in a manner that prevented him from practicing independent living in the context of the SPILST Program living quarters.

Collaboration between the Detroit Police Department and Don Bosco Hall was important in keeping Bayco from being incarcerated for carrying a sawed-off shot gun. Everyone at Don Bosco Hall was very surprised that Bayco had performed such a criminal act. According to the supervisor, when he asked Bayco to explain his reasons for carrying the weapon and whether he indeed intended to commit the act of car-jacking, Bayco stated that he had the sawed-off shot gun so that he could rob drug dealers and give the money to the poor people. He also talked about getting money for an item that he needed. At the time he did not identify the item he needed.

To the researcher, it seemed as though Bayco was taking actions in his own hands that he felt might have impacted drug trafficking in the City of Detroit. While Bayco's intentions might have been good, the way in which he carried out his plans could have led to his imprisonment for carrying a concealed illegal weapon. Additionally, the way in which Bayco decided to get money that he needed could have gotten him in trouble. It seemed as though Bayco would benefit from gaining knowledge and skills useful to realistically impact on drug trafficking in the City of Detroit. Bayco also needed to reestablish realistic goals for earning money to support his needs.

It would seem that an appropriate goal for Bayco at this point would be to assist him in developing appropriate advocacy skills and to gain insight into the consequences of carrying an illegal weapon. It seemed that Bayco needed to gain knowledge of appropriate methods that he might use to impact drug trafficking that severely and adversely impact so many members of his own sub-group. It seems that Bayco was fortunate that Don Bosco Hall was available to collaborate with the police officers and to advocate on his behalf. According to the literature review, unfortunately, more frequent than not, many low-income urban African-American male adolescents lacked such supportive agencies. Therefore, instead of them having second and third chances, they become a statistic in the criminal justice system.

JAY

This was the researcher's first interview with Jay. This interview was conducted at entry level into the SPILST Program. Questions were asked to obtain information about his personal history. The interview was conducted on the premises of the SPILST living quarters. During the interview Jay gave information about his personal and family history. Jay described himself as a medium height, medium weight, eighteen-year-old African-American male. Jay claimed that beginning at the age of eleven years old, he began to hang out on the streets and sell drugs. He said, "I never sold drugs to young kids, but young adults and older people were my customers. I had to make a living somehow, so I sold drugs so that I could make ends meet. But, selling drugs got me into trouble with my mother. As a result our relationship became poor and eventually I left home, took to the streets, and was homeless for about a month."

Jay stated that he never saw his biological father after his parents divorced, and he did not know whether his mother was living or dead. Jay states, "I believe that my mother died when I was eleven years old." Jay considered his family members to be his godmother, her husband, and their son. "My godmother is a white lady, but her husband is a black man. These people is my family now." Jay has spent a few nights with his godparents, yet they never took him in their home to live with them. Instead, Jay became a ward of the court system and began living in and out of residential group homes since the age of eleven.

At the age of thirteen, Jay was placed in the Don Bosco Hall SIL program. In this program he lived in a home with family members who had contracted with Don Bosco Hall to provide a foster care type living arrangement to Jay. Although he was under the supervision of a family, he was allowed to function as independently as possible. However, Jay abused these privileges. As a result he was returned to Don Bosco Hall's on site Residential Treatment Program.

Jay was not pleased about being returned to that living arrangement. As a result of his disappointment, Jay ran away from Don Bosco Hall and took to the streets again to be homeless and to once again sell drugs. His unstable living arrangement and his drug trafficking activities resulted in his being picked up by the police and being returned to Don Bosco Hall. He was in and out of Don Bosco Hall until the age of fourteen years old, and he sold drugs as a means of financial security.

Jay stated that, "By the time I reached sixteen years old, I became tired of selling drugs and hanging on the street corners. Most of the time, I didn't know whether I was going to live or die. I didn't care about anyone, and another thing, I couldn't have a meaningful relationship towards females. My only relationships with females were primarily sex related. I didn't do very well in school because I missed so many days out of school. Also doing most of my high school years, my grade point average was 2.5."

Interview with the Supervisor regarding Jay

This was the first interview at entry level with the Supervisor of the Transitional Services Program at Don Bosco Hall. During this interview the supervisor gave his opinion about Jay. "Yes, Jay has been homeless in the past and he has been part of the juvenile social services system. Homelessness for him began at age thirteen years old, due to a bad situation at home. From the period of leaving home, he often sold drugs in order to survive. As a result of his behavior, he became a ward of the Juvenile Justice System, Department of Social Services (MDSS), and the Foster Care System. MDSS placed him with Don Bosco's on-site Residential Living Facility. He has had some difficult times, but he has come a long ways. For that reason I believe that he will be able to fit well into the SPILST Program living quarters."

From the information obtained from Jay and the Supervisor of the Transitional Programs at Don Bosco Hall, the researcher concluded that it seemed as though Jay would be a good candidate for the SPILST Program. Although he experienced some challenges, the staff believe Jay deserved an opportunity for a chance to practice independent living in the least restrictive environment and as normal a setting as possible.

First Interview with Jay

During the first entry-level interview, Jay also discussed his past living experiences. Jay stated that he had never lived in his own apartment before this living arrangement. He said that he had always lived with other people and that he had never been responsible for managing his life or paying for anything that he needed. He said that Don Bosco Hall paid his rent from a subsidy received from the Michigan Department of Social Services. Additionally, Don Bosco Hall provided him with money to be used to get the utilities turned on in his name. Jay said that Don Bosco Hall also gave him a monthly allowance to be used to pay the utility bills and obtain personal items.

Jay added that he had to use money from his personal allowance for the installation of his telephone. Jay stated that he was proud to have his own apartment and that he planned to keep it clean. He acknowledged that he had a great deal to learn while living on his own. He stated that he needed to learn self-control as he could sometimes become physically aggressive when faced with stressful situations. Jay said, "I can be violent when I want to be. I don't start nothing. A lot of black males are violent against each other. The reason why is rage, I guess, rage against each other. They don't like themselves, therefore, they don't like you."

Jay went on to talk about his employment experiences. He said that he had been turned down on many occasions while seeking employment in the Detroit area. He said that he had knowledge of other racial groups being hired even though he had applied for the same job: "In those instances I felt that racial discrimination was practiced." He said that he had obtained

50

most of his minimum wage jobs with the assistance of Don Bosco Hall. He added that those jobs paid him no more than $4.25 per hour. According to Jay he had not looked for employment in the suburbs because of his lack of interest, difficulty that black young men experience while attempting to secure employment in the suburbs, and a lack of transportation. Jay went on to say that he had heard that jobs in the urban areas were limited. Jay stated that he felt that perhaps the lack of employment opportunities for African-American males were the results of the way they have been perceived by others. He said that his experience has been that females had gotten jobs more frequently than the African-American males. He also said that he felt that such was sexual discrimination rather than racial discrimination.

Jay reported that he felt that there were two important ways to secure job opportunities for African-American males. The first way, according to Jay, was that those who want jobs should travel to the suburbs to get them. The second way, according to Jay, was that African-American communities should create job opportunities within their own community. Jay went on to say that he felt that African-American male adolescents must clearly demonstrate that they want to work. For example, they must dress appropriately and communicate effectively.

Jay spoke about his interest in completing high school. He said that he intends to quit his part-time job in order to devote his attention to his academic assignments. He said that an adequate education would increase his chances of being successful. Jay said, "I just look at it like this. My education comes first and I am going to do whatever it takes to get my education straight. So when I am complete with that, I think I am successful. So, I have managed myself well. I have a good feeling about myself. This is just a stepping stone. This is half the way. You cannot do anything with only a high school diploma, you have to go further than that."

In the researcher's opinion, Jay was fortunate in that he was enrolled in a supportive community agency such as Don Bosco Hall, which provided financial means to support him while he concentrated on his education.

Jay continued with the interview and talked about his experiences with police officers. He said that he had some poor experiences with police officers. He reported, "In terms of being arrested by police officers, it has been terrible because the police ain't right, they always beating on you. I have been beat up by police officers. They beat me everywhere, the police, they don't care, they hit you on the strength of, because they want to. No, I was not badly beaten, I did not have bruises, but, pain here and there, they beat me with their hands."

Further, in the interview session, Jay stated that he felt that there were two very important factors in sharing a house with others. According to Jay, they were to mind your own business and manage your responsibilities. He stated that his living experiences had certainly been different while living in the SPILST Program as opposed to living in the SIL program with the family home providers. These differences, according to Jay, were that in the SPILST Program living quarters he had to learn to be responsible for himself and his surroundings. But in the SIL program he depended on others to care for him. Jay said, for example, "Just say that they give you a hundred dollars and I jack it off, then my lights and my gas will get cut off. But if you live in a group home, you could jack off the one hundred dollars, because those bills are automatically paid by the group home. Experiences in the SPILST Program teach you, if your gas and light gets cut off, that means the stove and refrigerator gets cut off, which you cannot have any food, so it's a lot of consequences following you. In the SPILST Program, it teaches you a lot of independence. The most independent skill I have learned since I have been here is how to budget money and how to self-discipline myself."

Second Interview with Jay

The second interview with Jay was conducted three months after he began to participate in the SPILST Program. Jay stated that he had been responsible for cooking for himself and he had friends over to his apartment for short visits rather than overnight. He emphasized that a skill that he had learned since living in the SPILST Program living quarters was to budget his money. He said that he had to learn the hard way. Jay went on to explain that his telephone was disconnected because he did not pay his telephone bill. He said that he had expected Don Bosco Hall to give him money to pay that bill. As a result it did not get paid. This resulted in a monthly increase in the telephone bill. Jay said, "I have learned from this lesson, from this situation, don't depend on anyone, depend on yourself and also pay your bills on time."

Jay talked about his employment experiences. He said that he had a job located in Detroit, Michigan. He reported that he got the job by filling out an application and the employer calling him. He said, "They called me, I didn't call them. I guess I was lucky that time because they have turned me down also, just because I am young and black." Jay discussed his thoughts on the reasons why African-American male adolescents have difficulties securing jobs. "I know that people discriminate against African-American young males because we are young and black. I also have another opinion. I believe that some young black men are lazy and they just don't go out to look for jobs. The availability of jobs for them is half and half. But to get jobs for them, I recommend that they look for a job. The community has to encourage them to get a job." Jay went on to say that dressing appropriately was important to getting a job. Jay commented that when a person gets a job they must be on time and do the job well. Having an agency like Don Bosco Hall to go with you to get a job is also helpful.

In terms of his school experiences, Jay mentioned that he enjoyed going to school. He further stated that he got along well with his teachers and peers. He added that one of the motivating factors that kept him in school was the "chicks." He also said that he wanted to make good grades. He reported, "I got to strive, ain't nobody here for me in this world. I am here by myself. The consequences for a lack of education is you can't get a job." Jay said that he wanted to devote time to completing high school so that he would have that task behind him. Jay went on to discuss how the SPILST Program has helped him. "I have a better sense of self. I know that I will stay away from the drug trafficking crime because I have an education and have gained a better opportunity to get a good job. I can work to earn a living now instead of doing the drug thing. This will keep me from getting involved in criminal activities. I think that living in the SPILST Program living quarters helped me with seeing what I wanted out of life. I thank you and Don Bosco Hall for this opportunity. Although, sometimes I say that Don Bosco Hall have not helped me, they really have bent over backwards to help me. One of the many things that they did was to help me to get enrolled in college. That was great."

Third Interview with Jay

By the third interview, which was six months after Jay's entry into the SPILST Program, Jay had left the SPILST Program living quarters and gone to a university located out of the Detroit area. While on semester break from that university campus, he stayed with his godmother, who lived in a suburb in Michigan. Therefore, the final interview took place in his godmother's home.

During the interview Jay stated that he enjoyed his visit with his godmother. However, he emphasized that his experience with the suburban police officers had been unpleasant and challenging to Jay. He stated that during his visit with his godmother, his first encounter with two white police officers occurred when two officers saw him at a restaurant located in the suburb. He reported that they approached him while he was standing at a telephone booth talking to the Supervisor of the Transitional Living Program at Don Bosco Hall. He said they wanted to know his reasons for being in that community. Jay reported that their voice tones sounded very aggressive. He said that he felt they did not respect his human citizen rights and demonstrated their disrespect for him by the manner in which they questioned him. Also, they had detained him for no apparent reason. He stated that after they could not find any reason for detaining him any longer, they finally allowed him to leave. He added that at that point he returned to his godmother's home where he felt safe.

Jay reported that the second time white suburban police officers approached him occurred when he was sitting in his godmother's car in front of a masseuse parlor as he was waiting to pick her up. The police officers approached him, pulled their guns out, made him put his hands on the car, and physically searched him. Jay stated, "I was only sitting in the car waiting for my godmother, who is a Caucasian woman. But as an African-American male adolescent in a community made up of a predominately white population, I looked suspicious to the white police officers. I was scared, I did not know what the police officers were going to do." Jay reported that his godmother happened to be coming out of the masseuse parlor at the time the police officers were confronting him. He said that his godmother intervened and confirmed his story. To that end, he was allowed to leave that location with his godmother.

Analysis by the Researcher

Jay had been known to have an aggressive temper when confronted with stressful events, but he was able to maintain self-control during the times he was approached by the white police officers of that suburban community. It was apparent that in that instance, Jay was able to maintain self-control.

There are two factors the researcher considered to be important to Jay's experiences. Firstly, Jay maintained self-control and secondly, his godmother intervened and advocated on his behalf. When the researcher considered Jay's experiences with the police officers, several questions came to the mind of the researcher. The first question was, "What would have happened to Jay had he spoken up for himself and had his godmother not been present to intervene on his behalf when approached by the police officers?" The second question was, "Did Jay have feelings of rage towards the police officers, but suppressed them for fear of severe punishment?" The third question was, "In the event that Jay felt rage and anger, in what manner would he have expressed his feelings?" The fourth and fifth question were, "Did Jay experience racial discrimination? Could a citizen complaint have been filed by Jay or his godmother against the white police officers?" A sixth question was, "How many low-income urban African-American male adolescents have been stopped by police officers for no apparent reason? Of that number how many have been arrested and incarcerated merely because they were African-American male adolescents? If they have been stopped for no apparent reason, how many would have been released had someone intervened and advocated on their behalf?"

"How many of those released would have had an opportunity to practice independent living? How many would have benefited from community service from a community agency?" None of these questions were answered in this case study but might be appropriate for future study.

Observation of the Supervisor of the Transitional Living Program at Don Bosco Hall

The supervisor indicated that the staff at Don Bosco Hall is very proud of Jay. He said that at the time that he entered the case study, Jay's interest in attending college was limited. But after he experienced living on his own, he realized that having an education was the key to his obtaining a job that might pay the kind of wages needed to support the kind of living habits Jay preferred. The supervisor indicated that the living arrangement in the SPILST Program helped Jay to gain skills needed to manage a home.

The supervisor further indicated that he felt that two incidents that occurred when the suburban police officers stopped Jay were institutional factors that impacted the way Jay saw himself and his environment. He further stated that had those incidents not been managed appropriately, they might have led to Jay's being incarcerated. The supervisor went on to discuss two incidents that occurred with Jay and the police officers. He stated, "They made him get out of the car, put his hands on the top of the car, and checked him. Jay said that they were aggressive towards him. He was scared, so he did not do anything. He handled himself well. Yet, both he and his godmother were upset about that incident. He felt that the police officers did not respect his human civil rights."

FRANK

The interview with Frank was conducted at entry level of his participation into the SPILST Program. During this first interview with Frank, he described himself and his personal and family history. Frank identified himself as a twenty-year-old, medium weight, medium height, African-American male young adult. During his early childhood development, he lived with his biological mother, who was diagnosed as mentally ill. Frank stated that he believed that she loved and cared for him as best she could, but during her episodes of mental illness, her ability to manage her child care responsibilities were limited. Frank stated that in some instances she was accused of neglect and abuse of him. He reported that these allegations resulted in the Department of Social Services removing him from his mother's home. Frank said that by the age of five or six, he became a ward of the court and was placed in a foster family home. He said that he was later moved because one of the foster family's sons sexually abused him. Frank reported that the foster family's son placed an electric cord under his arm and shocked him. He said that as a result of the shock, blisters formulated under his arm from the intensity of the shock.

He said that after this incident, he was returned to his biological mother. Frank reported living with her for one year, but his mother again experienced episodes of mental illness. This resulted in the Michigan Department of Social Services removing him from his mother's home and placing him in a boys' home. He said that he stayed in that home for a year, but after his mother became stabilized, he was allowed to return to his mother's home. Frank stated that after approximately one year living with his mother she again experienced an episode of mental illness. In that instance the Michigan Department of Social Services removed him from his mother's home and placed him in Don Bosco Hall Emergency Residential Program. Frank said, "My mother and I love each other, but she was just too sick to take care of me. I wish there had been some way someone could have come to live with us and help my mother take care of me. I should not have been taken away from my mother just because she was mentally ill, that wasn't right. After six months' stay in the Emergency Residential Program at Don Bosco Hall, my mother was allowed to visit me but was not allowed to take me home for visits. Upon my one year anniversary, I moved from that program to Don Bosco Hall's long term Residential Treatment Program. While in that program, I lived with foster parents and their five children."

Frank went on to say that he lived with the family for a year but had to leave because he was not willing to follow that family's rules and regulations. Because there were no other homes available, he returned to Don Bosco Hall Residential Treatment Program. Frank stated that he later changed his mind and finally decided that he could follow the home rules and regulations. His changed attitude resulted in his again being returned to that same family's home. He stated that he lived there until March 1993, at which time he agreed to participate in the SPILST Program living quarters.

Interview with the Supervisor regarding Participant Frank

This was the researcher's first interview with the Supervisor of the Transitional Service Program at Don Bosco Hall regarding Frank. Following are his comments about Frank's personal and family history. "No, Frank has never been homeless. In terms of Frank's school experiences, I know that when he was in grade school Frank had been labeled by the Detroit Public School system to be a learning disabled child. This label followed him throughout his high school years. This year, 1993, I questioned whether such a label was appropriate for Frank. The reason for my question is because when Frank took the Scholastic Aptitude Test at the end of this school year, he scored above average. I believe that if he had been a slow learner, he would not have scored that high on the SAT. One thing that may have contributed to Frank's low grade average in school was that he had poor vision, which, according to Frank, impaired his classroom participation. I wondered whether the system placed Frank in a category that was unjust and not true to his ability.

"Frank has been in the system for a long time because of alleged neglect and abuse by his mother. Unfortunately, his mother had emotional problems and could not manage child care. It would have been good if someone could have helped her with raising him. Although Frank has had his ups and downs, he has progressed well and the staff at Don Bosco Hall felt that he would be a good candidate for the case study project."

Following the interview with Frank and the supervisor, the researcher also concluded that Frank seemed to be appropriate for practicing independent living in the SPILST Program living quarters.

First Interview with Frank

During the first interview, Frank also discussed his experiences at entry level into the SPILST Program. Frank reported that this was his first time living in his own apartment. He said that he had never before looked for an apartment. Nor had he earned enough money to pay for an apartment. Frank stated that he was very appreciative that Don Bosco Hall had the responsibility of securing living arrangements and paying rent for him. When asked about low-income housing for individuals of his age range and sub-group, Frank stated that he felt that there should be low-income housing available to adolescents so they would not have to be out on the streets or involved in violent crimes in order to get enough money to find a decent place to live. He also stated that he felt that more landlords should rent to teenagers.

Frank added that prior to being placed in the SPILST Program living quarters that he had lived in Don Bosco Hall's SIL program with the home providers. He said that in those living arrangements he felt that most decisions were made for him by someone in the agency or the home provider. He said that he felt he was told when to get up, when to go to bed, where to go, and when to return as well as what he should eat. He went on to say, now that he was in his own apartment in the SPILST Program, he was responsible for making his own decisions about his life. He stated that decisions made by him must lead towards

59

progress based upon goals and objectives of him being in the SPILST Program living quarters and Don Bosco Hall.

Second Interview with Frank

The second interview was conducted three months into Frank's participation in the SPILST Program. By the second interview, Frank stated that he had been discharged from the Michigan Department of Social Services (MDSS) because he had reached the age of twenty, which was the eligibility limit. He said as a result of his reaching the age of twenty, MDSS could not justify reasons to keep him on their case load. He added that as a result the housing subsidy that had been provided to him from MDSS had terminated. He stated that at that point his medical coverage was in jeopardy unless Don Bosco Hall could convince the MDSS to maintain his medical coverage until he had secured another means of obtaining such. According to Frank, fortunately, Don Bosco Hall continued their support for an extended period of time after he had been terminated from MDSS.

Frank said that since MDSS had officially discharged him from the state juvenile court ward, the rules and regulations that once governed him through Don Bosco Hall relationship no longer existed. He reported that he was now an independent person and could choose whether he wanted to continue to be involved in the case study and whether he wanted to continue to follow the rules and regulations that governed the other three participants involved in the case study. After some consideration Frank stated that he would continue to follow the rules and regulations and would remain involved in the case study.

Frank stated that after a few months without sufficient financial subsidy from MDSS, Don Bosco Hall had no choice but to officially discharge him from their program. However, unofficially they continued to provide supportive community services as he continued to need supportive services and supervision.

He reported that after Don Bosco Hall officially discharged him from their program, he moved from sharing an apartment with one of the participants to an apartment on the second floor of the apartment in the SPILST Program living quarters. Frank stated that since he had been living on the second floor, he had been victimized. He said, "After I moved to the second floor, my apartment was broken into three times. I suspected that the robberies were committed by one of my peers who shared the same apartment building or my peer's friends. The second time that I was victimized occurred while walking in the neighborhood where my girlfriend lived." He said, "Three African-American males rushed out of a car and physically attacked me for unknown reasons to me." Frank added that although he was bruised, he did not receive any broken bones. Frank described another occasion when he was robbed. He said that in that instance his leather coat was taken at gun point. He stated that he was frightened but not physically harmed. He described yet another incident of robbery that occurred at a bus stop after he had cashed his check. He stated that during the robbery, his jaw was broken and as a result, he was hospitalized and treated for his broken jaw. He said that after all of these incidents, his feelings of victimization increased. Since that time he had avoided being away from his apartment after dark.

Third Interview with Frank

The third interview was conducted six months after Frank first began to participate in the SPILST Program. Frank stated that he had just completed high school. He said that he was so proud of himself. He acknowledged that completing high school was a challenge to him, but he felt a great sense of accomplishment and relief. "It would have been helpful had my teachers showed that they had expectations of me. I think that I would have put forth more effort had they shown me that they cared about me. But because I was in special education classes, people considered me to be dumb anyway. I had one teacher who supported me. That made me feel good."

Frank said that during, his freshman and sophomore years, he was doing good, but in the eleventh and twelfth grade, his grade point average began to decline. He stated, "I guess I had a few bad times. I had a poor attitude, so to speak, I cared, but

I did not put efforts in it. I was kind of lazy. Then after my senior year, I graduated because it was a make me or break me situation. I decided that if you do not have an education nobody would support you. You have to go to school. I guess for me things changed personally, such as, I had a lot of low self-esteem and problems that affected how I felt towards school. In terms of increased interest in graduating, I changed from bad to better after my mother died. It gave me more a burst of energy, to thrive to finish school. My family only had four people to finish high school. My mother wanted me to complete school. She wanted to come to my graduation, but she could not come because she had died. I did not want to let her down or my father, even though I didn't know him well."

Frank discussed his employment experiences. He said that he had been turned down on many occasions. "In such instances I felt that I was discriminated against because of my gender and race. I know of other situations where other black young men have been turned down for employment. But some other non-black kids get the job. This is not right." Frank went on to report that he has had three different job experiences since he first began working. "Two of them were obtained with the assistance of Don Bosco Hall. On many occasions Don Bosco Hall have gone on job interviews with me. They have advocated on my behalf and that helped me to get the job."

Frank reported that he experienced several personal losses during the past year. For example, his mother and father had died. Frank stated that he felt sad but was able to manage his stress. He mentioned that he sought support from Don Bosco Hall. As a result they provided services to help him cope with his stress. He added that he had been looking forward to new experiences. He said, "I look forward to owning a car of my own because I have never owned a car in my lifetime. I look forward to getting my driver's permit and license."

Observation of the Supervisor of the Transitional Living Program at Don Bosco Hall

The supervisor stated that Frank had been involved with Don Bosco Hall since he was five years old. He stated that he had watched him improve over the years since he was in the SIL program, but he noted a greater degree of independent living skills since he had been living within the context of the SPILST Program living quarters. The supervisor stated that he felt that Frank had taken the initiative to get up and arrive at school on time. He had been trying to keep his room clean, budget his money, and shop economically. He explained that Frank had received an inheritance and that he had used that source of financial support to manage his living arrangement and all of his needs. He stated, "If Frank had not received this financial resource from an inheritance, I don't know how he would have made it, since MDSS terminated him from their system."

The supervisor explained that as a child Frank had been labeled as learning disabled, but he questioned this labeling of Frank. He asserted that, "Recently when Frank took the Scholastic Aptitude Test (SAT), he scored high on the test. I believe that if Frank had been a slow learner, he would not have gotten such a high score on the test. I believe that society needs to look much more closer at the methods used to test our African-American male adolescents and other ethnic groups."

The supervisor discussed the incidents in which Frank needed to exhibit assertive behavior. He added that often he was judged by others as "slow" and had often been a target of criminal activities. He said that Frank had been robbed several times within the past six months. Therefore his guess was that Frank was perceived by others as being helpless and slow. He commented that Frank is an intelligent young man. "We at Don Bosco Hall are proud of Frank and encourage his continued success." He stated that the staff at Don Bosco Hall would continue to support Frank's effort to reach a greater level of independent functioning.

Analysis by the Researcher

During the past six months, Frank had shown progress. He had finished high school and was able to manage his apartment. Frank discussed his feelings about being victimized and an attempt to work through his feelings of victimization. However, he continued to avoid traveling by public transportation after dark in his community.

BILL

This was the first interview with Bill at entry level into the SPILST Program. In this interview, Bill offered limited information about his personal and family history. The following is a summary of his report.

Bill stated that he was an eighteen-year-old, small-framed average height African-American male. He was the oldest of three sisters and four brothers. He said that he grew up with his parents and siblings. They all got along well until he reached the age of fourteen. He reported that his problems with his family began when his father held him responsible for the behavior of his younger siblings. He said, "My father would physically punish me when I did not keep my sisters and brothers from getting into mischief. I could no longer tolerate my father's physical abuse, so at age fourteen and a half, I ran away from home and was on the streets for a few days. One day I was noticed by the police, who picked me up off the streets and took me to Don Bosco Hall's Residential Treatment Program. I lived there until I was promoted to the Semi-Independent Living (SIL) program, where I lived with a home provider."

Bill reported that he was unmotivated to attend high school. His lack of motivation prompted staff at Don Bosco Hall to encourage him to take the GED test. To that end, he took and passed the GED test. After receiving a GED certificate, Bill applied and was accepted in an educational program at one of the universities located in Detroit, Michigan. Additionally, he secured a part-time job, and he took part of his earnings to open a savings account at a local bank. Bill's demonstrated progress towards independent living functioning was an asset, which led to his being placed in the SPILST Program living quarters and his participation in the case study.

Interview the Researcher Had with the Supervisor regarding Bill

This was the researcher's first interview with the Supervisor of Transitional Services Program at Don Bosco Hall. He stated that he could not offer much information about Bill's personal and family history at this time. The following are the supervisor's comments: "Bill basically had a pretty good relationship with his family, but felt that his father put a great deal of responsibility on him for managing his siblings. No, Bill has never been considered homeless. When he was not living at home with his family, he lived in Don Bosco Hall's on site Residential Facility or with a home provider contracted to house young adults registered to Don Bosco Hall. Bill seemed pretty responsible for himself. Additionally, he usually avoided getting in trouble. Bill is a shy kid and often keeps to himself. He often visits his family members or make telephone calls to them. He recently got his GED and is currently attending a local university. Additionally, he was employed part-time. He has never lived on his own and could benefit from the SPILST Program."

After the researcher's interviews with Bill and the supervisor at Don Bosco Hall, it seemed as though Bill could benefit from practicing independent living skills at the SPILST Program living quarters and participation in the case study.

First Interview with Bill

This was Bill's first interview at entry level into the SPILST Program. Bill stated that this was his first time living in his own apartment. He said that he had never had to secure an apartment or be responsible for paying rent. He stated that he had looked in newspapers in the rental section merely to find out the cost of renting an apartment. To that end, he found that the cost of renting an apartment was very high. He stated, "I would like to see low-income housing for adolescents so they can maintain their apartment on their low-income wages." He felt that if such houses were available, teenagers would not have to hang around on the streets. He suggested that instead of the government having unoccupied houses torn down, they could have them repaired and made into low-income houses. He felt that the community could also assist by buying the abandoned houses and fixing them up for low-income houses.

Bill stated that since living in the SPILST Program he had become budget conscious. For example, he turned off his lights, TV, and radio when not in use. In addition, he would cut coupons from the newspapers and use them to lower his food bill.

Bill stated that he was happy to share the SPILST Program living quarters with other adolescents from Don Bosco Hall. He felt that it was much easier to share an apartment complex with persons he knew instead of strangers. He also stated that he felt that if he lived in an apartment alone, he would go "crazy." He emphasized that with everyone living in the same complex, they all kept an "eye" out on each other's personal property. Additionally, they were support systems for each other.

Bill went on to say that he felt things would work well at the home as long as everyone cooperated with each other. Bill reported that this was his first experience negotiating with the utility and telephone companies to have services turned on in his name. Bill talked about his attempts to find jobs. "I have been turned down on many occasions. Black males have a hard time finding jobs not only in the city of Detroit but particularly in the suburban cities. If you are black and a male, you can just about forget about it. People discriminate against you. Yes, I have been discriminated against by potential employers. To help me out, Don Bosco has gone on job interviews and waited for me until the interview was over. Yes, Don Bosco Hall has helped me to get a job. I have never gotten a high technology job because I just don't have the skills. As a result I have not tried to compete for high technology jobs. I feel that early on in the course of my high school years I should have been involved in classes that taught high technology skills."

Second Interview with Bill

This interview was conducted with Bill three months after he began participating in the SPILST Program. By the second interview, Bill behaved in a manner that indicated that he had decreased his sense of responsibility. For example, he admitted that he had mistakenly neglected to register for classes at the university, but had attended classes at the university an entire semester before he found that he was not officially registered. "I know that I should not have messed up. I thought about how Don Bosco Hall had helped me to get into the university by meeting with them and working things out for me. So I should not let them down. Besides, if I mess up again, I wondered if they would help me out again. I said to myself I will do better next time, I will make sure that I am registered for the classes."

Bill stated that Don Bosco Hall had become concerned about his behavior. He said, "For example, I had a problem with one of the guys living in the apartment. We got into a fight one day. The fight started when I went to his room to get some of his cassette tapes. He asked me to leave out of his apartment. So, I told him to make me. He started pushing me out of his place. I finally left his place and went to my place. He thought that I had taken some of his tapes, so he came to my place to get them and that was when the fight started. The other guy that stayed down on the first floor came up and stopped us from fighting. They called Don Bosco Hall and they came to see what was going on. After they arrived they told us not to fight but to call them if we could not settle our disagreements. Since that time, I don't say much to the guy. Next time I will call the police so he can get into trouble."

Bill admitted his lack of responsibility for himself and his difficulties managing conflict jeopardized his living in the SPILST Program and increased his chances of being returned to the SIL program. Bill stated that he was approached by Don Bosco Hall regarding his behavior. He said, "They encouraged me to improve my behavior or be put back in the SIL program." He added that after a few days had passed, he showed improvement. To that end, Don Bosco staff decided not to move him from the SPILST Program living quarters. Instead they increased monitoring and supervision of his behavior. Bill stated that he experienced consequences for his behavior, in that he was moved from his single one-bedroom apartment, to the first floor of that same building. He stated that in that living arrangement, he shared the apartment with the live-in manager. He stated that the live-in manager was new to the apartment.

Third Interview with Bill

By the third interview, Bill was involved in another incident that could have had an adverse effect upon him remaining in the SPILST Program living quarters. Bill stated that the incident happened on his birthday. He reported that he had gotten intoxicated and became verbally aggressive towards the live-in home manager, who was an African-American male student assigned to the SPILST Program living quarters by Don Bosco Hall. Bill stated that as a result of that incident, the live-in home manager called the police. Bill went on to say, "When they came, I was arrested and taken to the police station for a few hours. But I was released and returned to my apartment. I was mad at first, but the police officers kept me at the police station until I cooled off. So by the time I got home, I had calmed down and regained self-control." Bill stated that the live-in home manager had called Don Bosco Hall, and they came to the apartment. He said that they told him that his behavior was unacceptable and was not to occur again. They instructed him on the appropriate manner to vent his frustration.

Analysis by the Researcher

As indicated in the above paragraphs, Bill had behaved aggressively toward one of the other participants. As well as on another occasion, he had behaved aggressively toward the live-in house manager. As a result of Bill's behavior, Don Bosco Hall began to monitor Bill more often as opposed to removing him from the SPILST Program living quarters. Additionally, after a period of time, as Bill demonstrated that he could manage his behavior, Don Bosco Hall decreased the frequency of monitoring him. At that time their strategy was to affirm Bill's positive behavior and coach him on conflict management skills. It appeared as though Don Bosco Hall wanted to give him another chance to improve his conflict management skills. In this way he could rely more on his own initiative and sense of self-control. It seemed as though they wanted to empower Bill to manage himself and put greater emphasis on performing activities conducive to him gaining a greater sense of independent functioning, rather than behaving aggressively as a means of managing disagreements.

Observation of the Supervisor of the Transitional Living Program at Don Bosco Hall

"Bill has come a long way. He was a high school dropout. But, we at Don Bosco Hall encouraged him to get his GED. After getting his GED, he registered to attend one of the local universities. Now, he is getting ready to go out of the city to another university." The supervisor stated that in reflecting back on Bill's experiences, he had been doing well in school while he was living in the SIL program with a home provider. Yet, since he had been living in the SPILST Program living quarters, Bill had occasionally demonstrated a lack of responsibility in attending college as well as related activities. In addition, Bill had been verbally aggressive towards Don Bosco Hall's live-in house manager. As well as, Bill had been physically aggressive towards one of his peers who was also participating in the case study.

Finally, the supervisor explained that they had begun to wonder whether giving Bill such a level of freedom was conducive to his increasing his sense of independent functioning. He stated, for example, Bill had begun to have problems managing his apartment, budgeting, and understanding the importance of getting an education. He went on to say, "Just as we had told all of the other participants, we have also told Bill that it was very important to get an education and gain independent living skills."

SUMMARY OF THE INTERVIEWS WITH EACH PARTICIPANT AND THE SUPERVISOR AT DON BOSCO HALL

After conducting these interviews, the researcher better understood each participant's personal and family circumstances. While their personal family experiences were important, these were not the experiences of focus during the case study. Instead, the central focus was the contemporary institutional factors that impacted these participants' efforts to reach independent lifestyles.

The case illustrations that are included in this chapter contain the participants' reports of their experiences during the six-months' case study. The study was conducted between the months of March 1993 and August of the same year. The sequential and chronological organization of these case illustrations provided a format for the researcher to manage the data collected from interviews with the participants. The case illustrations included data collected from the participants. Data collected through separate face-to-face interviews with each of the participants, consisted of descriptive reports of their own interpretations and analysis of their experiences as they practiced independent living skills while residing in the SPILST living quarters. In addition, they described their experiences as they also received supportive community services from Don Bosco Hall. Quotations from the participants were included, in hopes to make it possible for readers to get a cogent picture of the participant's experiences.

Reports made by the Supervisor of the Transitional Living Program at Don Bosco Hall were also included. In some instances his reports included contrasting interpretations of the ways in which he interpreted their experiences as opposed to the participants' interpretations. Additionally, he gave his opinion about the institutional factors impacting their efforts to reach independent living functioning. Further, he described services provided by Don Bosco Hall to assist the participants in their efforts to reach a greater degree of independence than they had at entry into the case study. Quotations from the supervisor were included to replay his exact remarks about his opinion of the participants' independent living experiences.

The researcher's analysis of the data collected was included to give an interpretation of each participant's efforts to reach an independent lifestyle. Also included was the researcher's analysis of the impact that institutional factors, including unemployment and unequal educational opportunities, had on their efforts to reach independent lifestyles. Additionally, a description of services provided by Don Bosco Hall to assist these participants in their efforts to reach independence was also included.

The researcher hoped that a detailed case study of this small group of low-income urban state juvenile court-ward African-American adolescents might provide information on how institutional factors impacted these participants' efforts to reach independence. In addition, the study might provide an understanding of the activities they need to be engaged in their efforts to reach independence. Further, it might provide an understanding of the kinds of supportive community services that could assist them to reach independence.

Criteria for Interpreting the Study's Findings

Criteria for interpreting the findings were developed from the review of relevant literature that defined adverse unemployment opportunities and unequal educational opportunities. All of the possible criteria that may have contributed to the four participants' adverse experiences were not included in the criteria due to the amount of time it would have taken to gather such data. Pattern matching/linking the data to the case study propositions have been shown by placing a check mark in the participants' box who was most impacted by the criteria. Participants who met at least three criteria were adversely impacted by the criteria.

The following pages contain tables that address specific research questions involving the adverse factors thought to impact the participants' efforts to reach independent lifestyles.

Table #1

Study Question:

How do adverse institutional factors, such as unemployment, impede African-American male adolescent efforts to reach independent lifestyles?

Criteria For Interpreting the Study's Findings	Bayco	Jay	Frank	Bill
High unemployment rate contributes to high drop out rate from the educational system.				X
Involvement in criminal activities as an alternative to employment opportunities.	X	X		
Experiences discriminatory hiring practices.	X	X	X	X
Lack of work skills to compete for high technology employment opportunities.	X	X	X	X

Table one supports the contention that adverse employment opportunities significantly impacted all of the participants' efforts to reach independent lifestyles.

Criteria in table # 1 were developed from assertions from Akbar, N. (1991). p.1; Britt, C. L. (1994). pp. 99-108; Chiricos, T. G. & Bales, W. D. (1991). pp. 701-723; Gibbs, J.T. (1988). pp.6, 10, xiv, 21, 23, & 245; Gray, D. (1991). pp. 10, & 24; Hill, P. Jr. (1992). pp.44-45; Joe, T. (1987). p.295; Magura, M. & Shapiro, E. (1987). pp.57-67; Sum, A. & Fogg, N. (1990). pp.47-55; & Wilson, A. N. (1991). pp.6-7.

Table #2

Study Question:

How do unequal educational opportunities impede African-American male adolescent efforts to reach independent lifestyles?

Criteria For Interpreting the Study's Findings	Bayco	Jay	Frank	Bill
Disproportionate number of African-American male adolescents are likely to be placed in special education/low tracking.			X	
African-American male adolescent experience low expectations by public school teachers to achieve academic excellence.			X	
Disproportionate number of African-American male adolescents experience high drop out rate from high school.				X

Table number two demonstrates that data collected through interviews did not support the assumption that unequal educational opportunities had a significant impact on the four participants.

In table # 2 the participants' experiences were matched with the criteria that most impacted their efforts to reach independent lifestyles. Criteria in this table were developed from the assertions from Ascher, C. (1991). p.6; Boutte, G.S.(1992). pp.786-789; Brodbelt, S. (1991). p. 387; Gibbs, J.T. (1988). pp. 78, 81, 238; Gray, D. (1991). p.19; Hilliard, A. G. 111. (1992). pp. 168-173; Kunjufu, J. (1989). pp. 33-43; & Leake, D. & Leake, B. (1992). p. 784.

Table #3

Study Question:

How does supervised practice independent living skills training improve the African-American male adolescent efforts to reach independent lifestyles?

Criteria For Interpreting the Study's Findings	Bayco	Jay	Frank	Bill
Increase self-reliance.	X	X	X	X
Decrease risk for involvement in criminal activities.	X	X		
Improve home management skills functioning.	X	X	X	
Increase socialization and social relationship skills.	X	X	X	X
Increase conflict management skills.	X	X	X	X

Table number three showed that these criteria had a significant impact upon the participants' efforts to reach independent lifestyles.

Criteria included in table # 3 were developed from the efforts of the researcher and representatives from Don Bosco Hall. Criteria were based on the objectives of the Supervised Practice Independent Living Skills Training Program. The independent living skills training criteria most important to subject's improved lifestyle were matched with the appropriate subject. A check mark has been placed in the box of the subject most impacted by the criteria.

Table #4

Study Question:

How do public supportive community services assist in the achievement of independent lifestyles of African-American male adolescents?

Criteria For Interpreting the Study's Findings	Bayco	Jay	Frank	Bill
In-home individual and group practice activities through assisting, directing and guiding service.	X	X	X	X
Establishment of relationships with potential employers.	X	X	X	X
Make job referrals and placement.	X	X	X	X
Provision of supervision through scheduled and unscheduled home visits and 24-hour telephone availability.	X	X	X	X
Accompany individual during employment interviews, meeting school officials, etc.	X	X	X	X

Table number four revealed that all four participants were significantly impacted by the criteria listed. Its indications held up the position that supportive community services had a significant positive impact on the participants' efforts to reach a greater level of independence than they had when they entered the case study.

Criteria included in table # 4 were developed from the efforts of the researcher and representatives of Don Bosco Hall. Criteria were based on the training methods that were practical in nature and that were most often provided through face-to-face contacts. Methods that were most important in assisting the achievement of independent lifestyles of each participant have been included. A check mark has been placed in the box of the subject most impacted by the criteria.

Table #5

Study Question:

How will advocacy techniques conducted by the public supportive community agency on behalf of African-American male adolescents decrease adverse impacts of institutional factors on their efforts to reach independent lifestyles?

Criteria For Interpreting the Study's Findings	Bayco	Jay	Frank	Bill
Collaboration with the Detroit Police Department created opportunities for second and third chances to avoid incarceration.	X			X
Collaboration with home provider created opportunities for second and third chances to comply with home rules and regulations.		X	X	
Collaboration with universities increased the opportunities for the participants to enter college.	X	X		X
Collaboration with potential employers increased the participants' opportunities for employment.	X	X	X	X

Table number five indicates that advocacy techniques conducted on the behalf of the participants by a supportive community agency had an impact on the institutional factors affecting their efforts to reach independent lifestyles.

Criteria included in table # 5 were developed from the efforts of the researcher and representatives of Don Bosco Hall. Criteria were based on the training methods that were practical in nature and conducted on the behalf of the participants. A check mark was place in the box of the subject most impacted by the criteria.

FIVE
Discussion and Conclusion

This study revealed that while adolescence is a very difficult period for African-American males in low income urban areas, the transition to adulthood can be more successful when there is a support system that assumes the socializing role of the family and the larger society. Historically, in the Black community, a community support system has been known as an "Extended Family." Such a family is important when the biological family is not present or when the family system does not function adequately. The collaboration between an independent home provider and a community service agency provided this kind of extended family support for four African-American youth at a critical moment in their development. All of the participants had been frequent wards of the court during their childhood because of neglectful and abusive family situations. Few of their daily experiences were preparing them for independent living lifestyles; instead their experiences appeared to the researcher to be reinforcing psychological and behavioral dependency. The study revealed that institutional barriers, impulsive behavioral responses and disappointments could create troubling experiences for the youth. For example, the experiences the youth had in the employment sector were consistent with the literature. They had trouble finding jobs, and when they found jobs, they were low paying.

According to Akbar (1992), Wilson (1991), Gibbs (1988) and Hill, Jr. (1992), a disproportionate number of African-American male adolescents experience unemployment as opposed to their white counterparts. Similarly, Magura and Shapiro (1987) reported that during the years of 1972–1984, the unemployment rate for these adolescents was 31.7 percent to 42.7 percent as opposed to 14.2 percent to 16.8 percent for their white counterparts. Likewise, Gray (1991) reported that in 1990 African-American male youth in the United States had an unemployment rate of 48 percent as compared to 25.9 percent for white male youth.

According to Kunjufu (1988) and Ascher (1991), far too many African-American male students are placed in special education. However, the finding in this study showed that only one of the participants had been impacted by criteria defined as adverse unequal educational opportunities. One example may not be symbolic, but when examining the Detroit, Michigan, figures alone, it is evident that a longitudinal study to examine the lives of African-American young men who are placed in special education is needed. Cited in the report entitled, the "Condition of Michigan Education 1992," the total number of students in special education was 157,464 in the 1991–1992 school year. This report did not separate the students by race and sex. However, a report in the Detroit Public Schools "Student Counts by Race and Sex" (1992) indicated that 7,450 males were in special education. Of that number 45 were native American, 17 were Asians, 101 were Hispanics, 615 were white and 6,672 were African-American male students. A Detroit Public School educational psychologist agreed with the researcher that the number cited in the report is still extremely high and is thought to support the assertion that labeling contributed to an adverse impact. One cursory observation about their schooling experience is that favorable schooling experience seems a matter of chance. Two students felt that they had supportive teachers, while for the other two students, school support system was inconsistent.

The third finding showed that supportive community services provided by Don Bosco Hall and the home provider were useful in helping the participants reach a greater degree of independence than they had when they entered the case study. In a like manner, advocacy techniques conducted by Don Bosco Hall staff, in conjunction with the Detroit police department, provided the participants with second and third chances to avoid serving jail or prison sentences. Even when their personal behavior placed them in jeopardy of making choices that were inconsistent with their educational and employment goals, advocacy roles provided by Don Bosco Hall and the home provider enabled these participants to have opportunities for second and third chances to reach independent lifestyles.

Finally, the findings revealed that practiced independent living skills helped these adolescents gain a greater sense of achievement and self-reliance. These skills were important to their increased level of independent functioning. Financial support provided by the Michigan Department of Social Services for the cost of their living arrangements, health care needs, and personal allowance was essential to their efforts to reach independent lifestyles. Such financial support allowed these participants to practice independent living skills without having to worry about the financial demands of daily living.

Supportive and affirming attitudes of Don Bosco Hall staff and the home provider were important to the participants gaining independent skills. The advocates realized a need for understanding and willingness to facilitate the participants working through alternative expressions of aggression. When it came to advocating on the participants' behalf, their understanding of the institutional factors impacting these adolescents and their sensitivity to the overall needs of these participants were important resources.

As indicated in chapter four, initially the participants were allowed the opportunity to capitalize on their own strengths as they practiced independent living. During that period, supervision was provided on an intermediate and infrequent basis. Toward the end of the case study, two of the participants began to break some of the rules and regulations governing their stay in the SPILST Program. The broken rules, such as no illegal weapons, no sexual activities or alcohol allowed on the premises, resulted in increased supervision of the participants by the agency. Removal of one of the participants became necessary to decrease the chances of disruption in the independent practice activities of the remaining three participants.

Despite the institutional factors faced by these four participants, they were able to complete high school studies. Three of the four participants enrolled in colleges located outside of the City of Detroit, Michigan. According to the supervisor of the Transitional Services Program at Don Bosco Hall, they have maintained good academic grades. The participant who did not enroll in college continued to reside in the SPILST Program living quarters after the study ended. He continues to work at being a responsible person.

Another significant finding was that a community-based program, in which a majority of the activities related to developing independent living skills using a practical frame of reference within the context of the living quarters, proved to be important as these adolescents worked to achieve independence. Liability to the home provider and the community-based treatment center were present when one of the participants kept a sawed-off shot gun in the SPILST Program living quarters. For example, when one of the participants allegedly brought a sawed-off shot gun into the living quarters, the risk of physical harm to the other participants presented a liability issue to the home provider and Don Bosco Hall. Instances of conflict between another one of the participants and the live-in home manager presented additional liability issues.

As a result of these liability issues, the need for alternative housing arrangements was readily apparent. The additional housing arrangements should include crisis residential homes to be used for emergency beds. These available beds would be used for adolescents who are responsible for a confrontational act to be temporally removed from the primary living quarters and immediately placed in a crisis residential home until that particular adolescent regained control over his/her aggressive behavior. In the instances when one of the participants and the live-in home manager were not able to resolve their disagreement, the participant could have been temporarily removed from the living quarters and placed at the crisis residential home. Without such available resources, the home manager called the police department, who then removed the participant from the home. After regaining self-control, he was allowed to return to the living quarters. But from that point through out the remainder of the case study, the participant voiced disappointment in having the police department involved in the settlement of their disagreement. This situation had a severe impact upon the relationship between the participant and the home live-in manager.

Getting the police involved and interruptions in the partici-pants'/home live-in manager's relationship may have been avoided had a crisis residential home been available.

As can be noted, three of the participants exhibited behavior that got them in trouble with the law. When exploring their reasoning for such behavior, they reported that they had not intentionally intended to behave in an unlawful manner, how-ever, they were attempting to survive in a world that presents itself as cold, uncaring, unjust, and adverse to them becoming productive law-abiding citizens. Their consensus was that car-rying an illegal weapon was a way of life to many black young men. Aggressive behavior towards each other was a form of gain-ing power and control over their environment. They reported that "fighting" their way through this world was what they knew best. They realized that their way of managing their lives often got them into trouble. They all felt that if they did not "fend" for themselves, who would?

IMPLICATIONS OF THE STUDY

One outcome from this study showed that adolescents can increase their level of independent lifestyles when given ade-quate, consistent supportive services as well as second and third chances in their efforts to become independent citizens in to-day's society.

Knowledge derived from the case study might encourage other local supportive community agencies to provide opportuni-ties for adolescents to live independently and learn from trial and error experiences to increase their independent lifestyles.

Human service systems involved with providing care to these adolescents must be sensitive and have knowledge of ra-cial, cultural, and ethnic issues that may arise while providing care to this group. These human service systems must be capa-ble of running interference, advocating on their behalf, and buff-ering them from adverse social and economic forces that impede their development and advancement towards independence. Ad-ditionally, the continuum of care of these adolescents must be flexible and supportive. Community systems involving educational and employment programs as well as the legal justice systems need to be willing to work cooperatively to help adolescents meet the challenges of institutional social forces that may impede their efforts to acquire independent lifestyles. These systems must allow adolescents to have second and third chances to try and fail and try again to gain independent living skills. From this study it seems that perhaps the most crucial issue policy makers might be confronted with is the effort to develop and implement collaborative comprehensive community-based services to allow economically disadvantaged African-American male adolescents to have hands-on practical experiences as they enter society. These programs should be designed to teach them independent living skills activities while also receiving supportive services from a community agency. Services designed to promote psychological and behavioral independence rather than dependence will have positive short- and long-term effects upon these young men as well as upon today's society. Psychological and behavioral independence for these young men increases their chances to become self-reliant and to gain the kinds of knowledge and skills conducive to improved economic conditions. Additionally, it decreases their chances of exhibiting the kinds of behavior that puts them at risk of involvement in the criminal justice and prison systems. Additionally, it decreases their motivation to remain dependent upon the welfare system.

RECOMMENDATIONS

1. Further research is needed to determine the extent that institutional factors and behavior factors have on the efforts of low-income adolescents reaching independent functioning.
2. Social workers and other professionals should advocate for the establishment of laws and policies that would allow service providers to provide independent living practices at the beginning of entry into their programs. Additionally, services should be provided to adolescents

82

beyond the age of twenty as long as their treatment goals warrant such length of services.

3. Professionals, community leaders, politicians, and other interested parties should advocate for local, state, and federal dollars targeted to build prisons to be redirected to supportive community agencies committed to teaching independent living skills to adolescents of all ages, genders, and ethnic backgrounds.

4. Conduct a longitudinal study to trace the lives of African-American young men who have been diagnosed learning disabled.

As Senator Donald Riegle, from Michigan, indicated in his opening statement at the U.S. Senate Committee on Banking, Housing and Urban Affairs, Washington, D.C. (1991):

The loss to society of unrealized potential and contributors and the human loss implicit in those members just ought to break the heart of any person who professes to have a humane attitude about what goes on in this country. So from a competitiveness perspective, as a nation, from a moral perspective, this problem has to be addressed and we've got to find a way to turn these trends around. (p.3.)

SUMMARY

This study revealed that even though the service provided by Don Bosco Hall helped to pave the way and run interference with institutional factors that impacted the struggle of these adolescents reaching independent living status, Don Bosco Hall efforts did not, however, eradicate the presence of these institutional factors. Unemployment, employment discrimination, underemployment, unequal educational opportunities, and unequal justice continue to exist in today's society.

The participants' description of their experiences as they practice independent living was much like that of far too many poor inner-city African-American adolescents. The difference in these adolescents as opposed to many other adolescents was that they were supported by a community agency and were provided with financial and health care resources from the Department of Social Services. These support systems were important to their reaching independent functioning.

During this six month study, the cost of operating the SPILST Program living quarters was $18,000 in actual spending. According to a report in the U.S. Department of Justice, Office of Justice Programs, Bureau of Justice Statistics (1990), in the state of Michigan, the operating expenses for incarcerating one inmate were $16,649 per inmate. The researcher estimates that had these same young men been incarcerated, the state of Michigan would have spent approximately $33,296 to house them in prison for six months. The cost of helping these adolescents gain independent lifestyles and being productive citizens in the state of Michigan was much less than it would have cost had they been incarcerated.

References

Akbar, N. (1992) *Visions for Black Men,* Winston-Derek Publishers, Inc., Nashville, Tennessee 37205, pp. 1, 6.

Ascher, C. (1991). "School programs for African-American male students." Trends and issues no. 15. Institution for Urban and Minority Education. ERIC Clearinghouse on Urban Education, 15, 6.

Bell, D. (1992, December 23). "Prisons are headed for crisis, Boss warns." Metro Edition. *Detroit Free Press,* p. 3A.

Bennett, C.E. (1991) "The black population in the United States: March 1990 and 1989." *Current Population Reports.* Population Characteristics Services. U.S. Department of Commerce, Economics and Statistics Administration Bureau of the Census. 448, 20.

Boutte, G.S. (1992, June). "Frustrations of an African-American parent: A personal and professional account." *Phi Delta Kappan,* 73, 787–788.

Britt, C.L. (1994, January). "Crime and unemployment among youths in the United States, 1958–1990: A time series analysis." American Journal of Economics and Sociology, Inc. *American Journal of Economics and Sociology,* 53 (1) 99–108.

Brodbelt, S. (1992, July/August). "How tracking restricts educational opportunities." *The Clearing House,* 64(6) 385–387.

Child Welfare League of America, *Standards for Independent Living Services* (1989). Child Welfare League of America, Washington, D.C.

Chiricos, T.G., Bales, W.D. (1991). "Unemployment and Punishment: An empirical assessment." *Criminology.* 29(4) 701–723.

Congressional Record, daily digest (1994, August 21). "Proceedings and debates of the 103rd Congress, Second Session." United States Government Printing Office. 140(120).

"Detroit Public Schools Students Counts by Race and Sex" (1993, April). Student information Systems Division of Information Services, Detroit Public Schools.

Duster, T. (1987). "Crime, youth unemployment, and the black urban underclass." Sage Publications. *Crime and Delinquency*, 33(2).

George, P.S. (1992). "How to untrack your school." Alexandria, Virginia: Association for supervision and curriculum development, pp. 3,8,9,27.

Gibbs, J.T. (1988) *Young, Black and Male in America: An Endangered Species.* New York: Auburn House. pp. xiv, xxii, 2, 4, 5, 6, 7, 10, 21, 23, 78, 81, 245.

Gray, D. (1991). "The Plight of the African-American Male. An Executive Summary of a Legislative Hearing, Accompanied by a Directory of Model Programs, Resources and Services." Michigan Consolidated Gas Company, pp. 10–26.

Hill, P., Jr., (1992) "Coming of Age, African-American Male Rites of Passage." *African-American Images,* Chicago, Illinois, pp. 18. 43, 44, 45.

Hilliard, A.G. 111. (1992). "The pitfalls and promise of special education practices." The Council for Exceptional Children, 59(2) 168–177.

Jankowski, L.W. (1992, July). *Correctional Populations in the United States, 1990,* U.S. Department of Justice, Office of Justice Programs, Bureau of Justice Statistics. p. 63.

Joe, T. (1987, April). "Economic Inequality: The picture in Black and White." Sage Publications, Inc. *Crime and Delinquency*, 33 (2) 287–299.

Jones, R.J. (1989) *Black Adolescents.* Berkeley, California, Cobb & Henry Publishers, p. 7.

Kean, P. (1993, January/February). "Blowing up the track: stop segregating schools by ability and watch kids grow." *The Washington Monthly.* 25(32), 33.

Kunjufu, J. (1989). "Critical Issues in Educating African-American Youth." (A Talk with Jawanza). Chicago: *African-American Images.* pp. 33–34.

Leake, D., and Leake B. (1992, June). "African-American immersion schools in Milwaukee: A view from the inside." *Phi Delta Kappan.* 73, 783–785.

MacCoun, R. and Reuter, P. (1992). "Are the wages of sin $30 an hour? Economic aspects of street-level drug dealing." Sage Publications Inc. *Crime and Delinquency.* 38 (4).

Magura, M. and Shapiro, E. (1987, Winter). "The Black Dropout Rate and the Black Youth Unemployment Rate: A Granger Causal Analysis." *The Review of Black Political Economy.* 15(2) 56–67.

Manning, M.L. and Lucking, R. (1990). "Ability grouping: Realities and Alternatives." *Childhood Education,* 66(4) 253.

86

Meisenheimer, II, J.R. (1990, November). "Black college graduates in the labor market 1979–1989." *Monthly Labor Review.* 113.(11) 13–21.

Michigan State Board of Education (1992). *Condition of Michigan Education.* News from the United States Department of Labor, Office of Information and Public Affairs, Washington, D.C. 20210. (1992, March). The Employment Situation: March 1992 Fillers from the U.S. Department of Labor. *Black News Digest.*

Obiakor, F.E. (1992). "Self-concept of African-American students: An operational model for special education." *The Council for Exceptional Children,* 59(2) 165.

Oliver, W. (1989). "Black Males and Social Problems Prevention through Afro-centric Socialization." Sage Publications. *Journal of Black Studies,* 20, 16.

Phillips, M.B. (1991). "A hedgehog proposal." *Crime and Delinquency,* 37(4) 555–574.

"Prison alternative shows people why there's hope they'll work." (1992, December 27). Edition: Sunday Metro Final Section (FP). *Detroit Free Press,* p. 2G.

Riegle Jr., Donald W. "Plight of African-American men in urban America, The." (1991). Hearing before the Committee on Banking, Housing and Urban Affairs, United States Senate, One Hundred Second Congress. United States Government Printing Office, Washington, D.C.

Smith, G.A. (1992). *Education and environment learning to live with limits.* State University of New York, p. 142.

Sniffen, M.J. (1994, June 2). "Inmate court nearly triples." Associated Press edition. Metro-Final Section: NWS(FP). *Detroit Free Press,* p. 4A.

State of Michigan Department of Social Services (1993, September). Wayne County Child Foster Care System Administrative Zone Office.

Statistical Abstract of the United States (1994). U.S. Department of Commerce, Economics and Statistics Administration Bureau of the Census.

Sum, A., & Fogg, N. (1990). "The changing economic fortunes of young black men in America." *The Black Scholar,* 21(1) 47–55.

Thomas, M.E. (1993, August). "Race, class and personal income: an empirical test of the declining significance of race thesis, 1968–1988." *Social Problems,* 40(3).

Wilson, A.N. (1991). *Understanding black adolescent male violence.* New York: Afrikan World Infosystems. pp. 6–7.

Yin, R.K. (1989). *Case Study Research Design and Methods*. Applied Social Research Method Series, vol 5. The International Professional Publishers. Newburg Park, London, New Delhi: Sage Publications. pp. 1–152.

Appendices

APPENDIX A
Explanation to the Young Adult

Hello, my name is Odeather Hill, and I am a learner in the Union Institute, which is located in Cincinnati, Ohio. My intention is to conduct a case study to inquire about your experiences prior to your entry into the Supervised Practice Independent Living Skills Training (SPILST) Project. I also intend to inquire about needs, feelings, problems, behavior, issues, and concerns that you have experienced since you entered the project. I will ask you to be interviewed, describing your experiences after you have become involved in the SPILST Project. I will need your permission to review your case files/records (if appropriate).

I will ask person(s) who are a representative of the supportive community agency of which you are registered to be interviewed. During the interviews these persons will be asked to give their opinions about your experiences under each category. These person(s) will give their opinions about your experiences from entry into case study project and three and six months post your participation in the case study project.

All interviews will be cassette-taped and kept for my files. These tapes will be transcribed and contained in hard-copy format. Information from these interviews will be used as the results of the case study.

My intentions are to publish your answers and the answers of the representatives of the supportive community agency. I will not write your name on any notes taken during the interviews. I am requesting that you do not write your name on any of the instruments so that your identity will not be made known. However, you will be asked to write your name on the consent form to participate in the case study. I will not identify you by name. I will not tell anyone that you have answered questions for me.

As a professional I will have to tell the proper authorities if you tell me that someone has been or is currently seriously hurting you.

During any time period, you can discontinue participating in the case study. All you have to do is let me know that you no longer want to participate in the research study.

In the event you consent to participate in this research study, please read and sign this consent form attached to this letter. When you sign this consent form, you are letting me know that you understand the intent of the study and agree to participate in the research study. At the beginning of each cassette-taped interview, you will also be asked to give your consent to the interview. This verbal form of consent may also be used as a form of consent.

Thank you.

APPENDIX B
Young Adult Consent Form

Name: _____

Years of Age: _____   Date of Birth: _____

Sex: (M) (F)   Race: _____

Socioeconomic Status: _____

1. I acknowledge that the research study on the Supervised Practice Independent Living Skills Training (SPILST) Program has been explained to me, and I understand that Odeather Hill, the researcher, will ask me questions about my needs, feelings, issues, consents, and problems prior to and after becoming involved with the SPILST Program.
2. I understand that for participating in the study I will not have to pay money.
3. I understand by signing this form that I am agreeing to participate in the research study on SPILST Program by being interviewed, observed, and casette- or videotaped. In addition, I will, identify problems, needs, behaviors, feelings, issues, and concerns related to my experiences prior to and after my involvement with the SPILST Program.
4. I agree to allow Odeather Hill, the researcher, to review my case files. I understand that I will not be identified by name.
5. I hereby acknowledge that Odeather Hill, the researcher, has fully and clearly explained to me the fundamentals of the research study. Further, Odeather Hill has explained that the data collected from the research study will be confidential and privileged information and I will not be identified by name.
6. I further understand that in the event I have any questions about the research study they can be directed to Odeather Hill, the researcher, or my worker at _____.
7. I am aware that I will continue receiving services from the _____ and that_____is an essential adjunct to

the Supervised Practice Independent Living Training Program. I further understand that if I discontinue participation in the SPILST Program, the_____ will remain available and such services are not dependent upon my remaining in the SPILST Program.

8. I hereby acknowledge that I have read the informed consent (or the contents of the informed consent have been explained to me) and I fully understand and agree with the contents of this document and research study. I acknowledge that I have been given a copy of this document for my files.

Name of participant: _____ Date _____

Age of Participant: _____ Time _____

Location where signature was signed: _____

Telephone:

_____ (Home) _____ (Work)

(Please check appropriate box below)

(   ) I agree to participate in the research study.

(   ) I agree to be identified as a study participant of the Supervised Practice Independent Living Skills Training Program.

(   ) I choose not to be identified as a study participant in the SPILST Program.

(   ) I decline to participate in the research study at this time.

Print Name of Participant	Date
Signature of Participant	Date
Print Name of Witness	Date
Signature of Witness	Date
Print Name of Witness	Date
Signature of Witness	Date
Print Name of Witness	Date

APPENDIX C

Psycho-social History Assessment

ID#: _____ Age: _____ DOB: _____ Date of Interview: _____

Informant(s)

Brief Statement of Problem:

Parental Information: (Please check appropriate boxes)

Parents are/were Married[   ] Never Married[   ]
Single [   ] Widowed [   ] Separated [   ]

Deceased [   ], if checked please indicate which parent. Father [   ] Mother [   ]

Other? Explain:

Were you reared by both parents? Explain:

What was your relationship with your parents? Explain:

Father:

Mother:

Sibling Information

Do you have any sister(s): Yes [   ] How many____ No [   ]

Do you have any brother(s): Yes [   ] How many____ No [   ]

Describe your relationship with your sister(s):

Describe your relationship with your brother(s):

Extended Family Information (Please check appropriate box[es])

Do you have persons in your family whom you consider to be support systems to you? Yes [   ] No [   ]

If yes, who are they: (i.e., grandmother, grandfather, cousin, uncle, aunt.)

Describe how they are your support systems:

If no, why do you not feel that they are support systems to you? Explain:

95

Development History

Did your mother have a normal pregnancy without major physical difficulties? Elaborate:

Did your mother have any emotional traumas in her life during her pregnancy with you? Elaborate:

Were there any difficulties during your delivery? Explain:

Socialization Experiences

For example, have you had any major problems getting along with others? Using leisure time, etc.? Describe:

Development Experiences

For example, did you have any major problems learning to sit, crawl, stand, walk, talk? Describe:

Educational Experiences

For example, have you had any major problems with reading, writing, mathematics? Describe:

Behavioral Experiences

For example, have you had major behavioral problems with peers, siblings, parents, schoolteachers, etc.?

Vocational Experiences

For example, have you have any vocational training and/or work experiences? Yes [   ] No [   ]

Describe:

Legal/Court Experiences

For example, have you ever been involved in civil, criminal, traffic cases? Yes [   ] No [   ]

Describe:

Self-Awareness

Describe your independence skills:

What do you consider are your strengths? Describe:

What do you consider are your weaknesses? Describe:

Your general attitude and behavior?

Worker's Impression

Participant's insight and judgment. Describe:

Participant's level of independent skills. Describe:

Participant's level of socialization skills. Describe:

Participant's level of educational skills. Describe:

Participant's attitude and behavior. Explain:

Status of person completing this form:

_____ Date _____

Name of Person Completing This Form

_____

APPENDIX D

Supervised Practical Independent Living Training Tool

Open-Ended Questions
001   Participant's ID Number:
002   Participant's Age:
003   Participant's Date of Birth:
004   Location of Interview:
005   Date of Interview:
Please check appropriate box below:
006   [   ] entry level
007   ]   ] 3 months post entry
008   [   ] 6 months post entry
Category Item: Housing
009   What have been your experiences in securing affordable low-income housing? Describe:
010   What have been the consequences of a lack of affordable low-income housing for you? Describe:
011   What do you feel can be done to increase the amount of affordable low-income housing for you? Describe:
012   What do you feel the community can do to assist inner-city black young adults who are seeking affordable low-income housing? Describe:
013   What have been your experiences in managing your current living situation? Describe:
014   What support systems have assisted you in securing affordable low-income housing? Describe:
015   What have been your experiences in sharing housing with others as you practice learning independent living skills? Describe:
016   What have been your experiences in paying rent for your housing quarters? Describe:

97

017 What have been your experiences in assessing your strengths and weaknesses in selecting adequate housing situations? Describe:

018 What have been your experiences in assessing and learning ways to manage yourself in an independent living situation? Describe:

019 What have been your experiences in identifying problems related to independent living? Describe:

020 What have been your experiences in identifying steps needed in solving problems faced with during independent living experiences? Describe:

021 What have been your experiences in saving money to pay rent? Describe:

022 What have been your experiences in understanding tenants' rights? Describe:

023 What have been your experiences in understanding the landlord's rights? Describe:

024 What have been your experiences in following health and safety standards? Describe:

025 What have been your experiences with your neighbors? Describe:

026 What have been your experiences in paying for utility costs in a timely manner? Describe:

027 What have been your experiences in preventing actions that may lead to eviction? Describe:

028 What have been your experiences in controlling behavior of guests? Describe:

029 What have been your experiences in responding to the landlord's complaints? Describe:

030 What have been your experiences in responding to the peers' complaints? Describe:

031 What have been your experiences in making minor repairs (i.e., putting in light bulbs, replacing screws in door knobs, etc.)? Describe:

032 What have been your experiences in the use of household appliances? Describe:

033 What have been your experiences in managing feelings of loneliness? Describe:

034 What have been your experiences in securing emergency medical or mental health services? Describe:

Category Item: Employment/Unemployment

035 What have been your experiences in your efforts to secure gainful employment within the past two years? Describe:

036 What have been your experiences finding employment in urban and suburban areas? Describe:

037 What have been your salary ranges during your employment experiences? Describe:

038 What do you feel are factors contributing to a lack of gainful employment opportunities for inner-city black male young adults? Describe:

039 What do you recommend to increase gainful employment opportunities for inner-city black male young adults? Explain:

040 What do you think the community can do to assist inner-city black male young adults who are seeking gainful employment? Describe:

041 What support systems have assisted you in securing gainful employment? Describe:

042 What have been your experiences in completing employment applications? Describe:

043 What have been your experiences in completing résumés? Describe:

044 What have been your experiences in dressing appropriately for employment? Describe:

045 What have been your experiences in complying with work hour requirements? Describe:

046 What have been your experiences in maintaining work habits? Describe:

047 What have been your experiences in relation to authority figures in the employment setting? Describe:

048 What have been your experiences in getting to the employment site in a timely fashion? Describe:

049 What have been your experiences in calling in to the employment site in cases where you have been unable to attend work? Describe:

050 What have been your experiences in safety factors during employment? Describe:

Category Item: Education

051 What have been your experiences in getting along with your peers at school? Describe:

Category Item: Health

052 What have been your experiences in securing health care services to meet your needs? Describe:

053 What have been your experiences in identifying health problems? Describe:

054 What have been your experiences in making appointments for health care needs? Describe:

055 What have been your experiences in keeping appointments for health care needs? Describe:

056 What have been your experiences in following medical recommendations? Describe:

057 What have been your experiences in practicing safe sex methods? Describe:

058 What have been your experiences in practicing good hygiene methods? Describe:

059 What have been your experiences in avoiding exposure of spreading health problems to others? Describe:

060 What have been your experiences in avoiding drug or alcohol use or abuse? Describe:

061 What have been your experiences in having knowledge of community health care services? Describe:

062 What do you feel are the consequences of the lack of adequate health care services for the inner-city black male young adult? Describe:

063 What do you recommend to increase adequate health care services for inner-city black male young adults? Describe:

064 What do you feel the community can do to assist in inner-city black male young adults receiving adequate care services? Describe:

065 Other:

Category Item: Crime and Delinquency

066 What have been your experiences in securing legal services to meet your needs? Describe:

067 What have been your experiences in being arrested by the police? Describe:

068 What have been your experiences in being accused of, or stealing, an item? Describe:

069 What have been your experiences in being accused of, or committing violence, against someone else? Describe:

070 What have been your experiences of being put in jail? Describe:

071 What have been your experiences with firearms? Describe:

072 What have been your experiences in being treated in a negative manner by security guards while shopping in a shopping mall? Describe:

Category Item: Socialization/Social Relationship

073 What have been your experiences in seeking opportunities for socialization? Describe:

074 What have been your experiences in developing meaningful relationships with the opposite sex? Describe:

075   What have been your experiences in maintaining meaningful relationships with the opposite sex? Describe:

076   What have been your experiences in making effective use of your leisure time? Describe:

Category Item: Recreational Activity

077   What have been your experiences with securing recreational activities designed to meet your needs? Describe:

078   What have been your experiences in attending recreational activities? Describe:

Category Item: Violence

079   What have been your experiences with violence? Describe:

Category Item: Transportation

080   What have been your experiences in having available to you the mode of transportation needed to travel back and forth from work or other destinations? Describe:

APPENDIX E

Consent Form for the Case Work Supervisor of the Transitional Living Service Program at Don Bosco Hall (Employee of Don Bosco Hall)

Name _____

Age _____ DOB _____ Sex _____ Race _____

I acknowledge that the research case study on the Supervised Practice Independent Living Training (SPILST) Project has been explained to me, and I understand that Odeather Hill, the researcher, will ask me to give my opinion about each participant's independent living experiences at entry level and three and six months post their participation in the case study project.

I understand that my opinion will be in response to questions under categories: housing, employment/unemployment, education, health care, crime and delinquency, socialization and social relationships, recreational activities, violence, transportation and any other issues, problems and concerns related to the participant's experiences.

I understand by signing this form that I am agreeing to participate in the research case study on (SPILST) Project by being interviewed, and that the interviews will be cassette-taped.

I acknowledge that Odeather Hill, the researcher, has fully and clearly explained to me the fundamentals of the research study. Further, Odeather Hill has explained that data collected from the (SPILST) Project research case study will be included in publication but will not include the names of the participants. I understand that my name and the name of Don Bosco Hall will be included in the (SPILST) Project research case study project and any publication.

I understand that in the event I have any questions about the (SPILST) Project research case study they can be directed to Odeather Hill, the researcher.

I acknowledge that I have read the informed consent (or that the contents of the informed consent have been explained to me) and I fully understand and agree with the contents of this document of the (SPILST) Project research case study. I acknowledge that I have been given a copy of this document for my files.

[   ] I agree to participate in the (SPILST) Project research case study.

[   ] I agree to be identified on the (SPILST) Project in the research case study.

[   ] I agree that Don Bosco Hall's name, contents of services provided (if needed) address, telephone number and any other related information can be included in the (SPILST) Project research case study and publications.

[   ] I choose not to participate in the (SPILST) Project research case study.

[   ] I choose not to be identified in the research case study.

[   ] I choose not to have Don Bosco Hall's name nor any other information be included in the (SPILST) Project research case study.

Name _____ Date _____ Location _____

Witness _____ Date _____ Location _____

APPENDIX F

Rental Agreement for Young Adults

The content of this document constitutes rental agreement. Breach of this rental agreement will result in the renter leaving the premises at _____.

    This is a rental agreement between_____, hereinafter known as "renter" and _____, hereinafter known as "landlord." The renter will reside in a _____ bedroom apartment where the rent will be $ _____ per month, to be paid to the landlord on the _____ day of each month. At the time of move in, the renter will pay the landlord one (1) month's rent and a security deposit equal to one month's rent (if appropriate).

    A thirty (30) day notice shall be made to the landlord in the event the renter decides to move from the premises.

    A thirty (30) day notice shall be made to the renter in the event the landlord decides the renter should leave the premises.

    Destruction of property is not allowed and is reason for immediate termination of this rental agreement. Any damage to the property at _____ is to be repaired by _____ within _____days of destruction of property.

    The renter is not to have loud music, parties, fights, or any other events that will disturb the residents at_____.

    Windows and doors are to be kept secure at all times.

    The renter will not be allowed to have high density traffic in and out of the premises at _____.

    The renter will keep a clean and orderly apartment.

The landlord will be responsible for all major repairs not resulting from damage caused by the renter. Any damage must be reported to the landlord immediately.

The renter must attend high school on a regular and consistent basis.

The renter must be willing to be involved in a work activity program.

The renter must maintain contact with his community support agency as needed.

The renter must pay all utilities (gas, water, electricity) in his own apartment and be responsible for his own food purchase, cooking, clothing and house cleaning.

The renter must be responsible for ordering and maintaining a telephone.

The renter must be willing to be involved in personal enrichment activities, such as enrolling in meaningful clubs, sport, attending church (optional), and participating in arts and crafts.

The renter is responsible for his own transportation. The renter (or anyone else) is not to have on property at_____ _____ any substance including illegal drugs or alcohol.

The renter is not to bring or allow anyone to bring firearms on the rented property.

The renter is not to intrude on the privacy of any persons living at _____.

_____ Date: _____
Print Name of Renter

_____ Date: _____
Signature of Renter

_____ DOB: _____
Age of Renter

_____ Date: _____
Parent/guardian signature (if youth is under 18 years of age)

_____ Date: _____
Print name of Landlord

_____ Date: _____
Signature of Landlord

Name of supportive community service _____ .
Name of supportive community service _____ .
Name of supportive community service _____ .
Name of supportive community service _____ .

About the Author

I was born in Luxora, Arkansas, and raised on a farm owned by a white plantation owner. I was the fourth child in a sibship of two sisters and two brothers. I never saw my biological father but was reared by my biological mother, Willie Lee Allen. I was five years old when my mother died of medical complications. However, after her death, my siblings and I continued to live on the same plantation, with my maternal grandmother and grandfather who took care of us. During that same year, my grandfather died. Two years later I experienced yet another loss when my second oldest sister died from medical problems, as well.

With the loss of my mother, sister, and grandfather, I had to help my grandmother, oldest sister, and oldest brother earn a living to support our family. We earned a living by chopping and picking cotton. During the spring and summer months, we chopped cotton, at which time we earned $1.35 per day. During the late summer and early fall months, we picked cotton for $.35 per hundred pounds. Our work day on the plantation began at 6:00 A.M. and ended at 6:00 P.M. or later. We worked in heat in which the temperature reached 107 degrees F. The sun was so hot that some of the workers fainted from sunstroke and exhaustion.

I grew up under conditions that were similar to those of my forefathers during the days of slavery. My family and other African-Americans had to say "no, sir" and "yes, sir" to all white people, no matter what their ages. We had to drink water from fountains marked "colored only," while whites were allowed to drink from any fountains of their choosing. We were not allowed to enter the part of the doctor's office that was identified for "whites" only. I remember watching white people beat Black men until blood ran down their faces. I recall feeling helpless and angry because of the way in which Black people were treated. On many occasions I felt sorry because my grandmother had to keep me from going to school so that I could go to the fields to chop and pick cotton so that the plantation owner's crops could be gathered during harvest season. I recall having felt cheated out of an opportunity to go to school to get an education. By the time I reached the age of seventeen, I got married, dropped out of high school, and moved to a big city in the western part of the United States.

Eleven months after I was married, I gave birth to my first son. After living in the big city for one year, my husband, my son, and I moved back to Arkansas. In order to help support my family, I began house-cleaning for one of the white families who lived in the community. I worked for the family until I became pregnant with my second child. While I was pregnant with that child, our family moved to Detroit, Michigan. By the time I was twenty-four years old, I had given birth to four children. Housewife and mother became my full-time career, and for many years I felt fulfilled. However, I later became disenchanted because I was unable to contribute to meeting the financial needs of my family. I did not have a high school education; the only job skills that I had were chopping cotton, picking cotton, and house cleaning. The disappointment that I felt motivated me to make positive changes in my life. As a result, in 1971, I purchased a set of GED books, studied the material, and successfully passed the GED test. Attaining an education was my first step to increasing my chances of helping me to meet the financial needs of my family. Since my early childhood, I had felt that obtaining an education would also increase my chances of making an impact upon institutional factors that perpetuate racism and injustice in this society. Determined to equip myself with the armor of education, in 1974 I enrolled in an associate degree program in a local community college. Managing the responsibilities of raising a family, being a housewife and a student were not easy tasks for me.

On many occasions I felt like giving up on reaching my educational goals. However, each time that I felt like quitting, I was reminded of a saying that my grandmother, Martha Alexander, often repeated when things got tough. She used to say, "Never give up on your dreams and never quit no matter how hard you have to work to meet your goals." Whenever I felt like quitting, the echo of my grandmother's words would sound in my mind. Another thing that helped me through was my drive to attain a higher education. This drive was so strong that I included the task needed to attain an education into my daily responsibilities of rearing my children. My hard work paid off. To that end, in 1976 I completed an associate degree program in Occupational Therapy from Wayne County Community College. I immediately began working as an Occupational Therapist assistant, but after working for two years, I resumed my education by entering a bachelor's degree program in social work at Wayne State University. For six months, I continued to work while attending the university, rearing my children and being a housewife.

Taking on so many responsibilities became overwhelming. As a result, I had to make a decision about whether to discontinue with working toward attaining the bachelor's degree or resigning from the employment position. Although working was important, attaining an education was more important to me. With this in mind, I decided to stop working until I earned the bachelor's degree. As a result of my hard work and effort, in the spring of 1981 I successfully completed the program. In the fall of 1981, I enrolled in an accelerated Master's Degree program in Social Work Administration at the same university. In 1982, I successfully completed that program. In 1987, I became a single parent. This was the first time in my life that I had to take full responsibility for myself. That experience was frightening while at the same time very challenging. Only one of my daughters lived with me at that time, but she soon became an adult and moved out on her own. I was no longer responsible for anyone other than myself, so I decided to invest my time and energy in earning a doctoral degree and to continue working a full-time job. In 1989, I enrolled in a non-traditional university. After six years of hard work, I earned a Doctor of Philosophy in Social Work. My dissertation was a case study of four young African-American men making a transition toward independent living. I examined the adverse institutional barriers that adversely impacted these young men's efforts to make a transition from young adulthood to adulthood. The result of the case study inspired me to write this book. The contents of this book will be useful to parents, professionals, paraprofessionals, teachers, young adults, political officials, community organizations, and others in their effort to assist young adults in making a transition toward independent living.